THE
BATTLE
BELONGS
TO THE
LORD

THE BATTLE BELONGS TO THE LORD

12 BIBLICAL REMINDERS THAT GOD FIGHTS ON OUR BEHALF

ELIZABETH VIERA TALBOT

Pacific Press®
Publishing Association

Nampa, Idaho | www.pacificpress.com

Cover design: Daniel Añez
Interior design: Aaron Troia
Editor: Aivars Ozolins
Illustrator: Kat Phan

The author assumes full responsibility for the accuracy of all facts and quotations as cited in this book.

You can obtain additional copies of this book by calling toll-free 1-800-765-6955 or by visiting AdventistBookCenter.com.

ISBN 978-0-8163-6795-5

September 2022

Dedication

This book is dedicated

to my husband, who is courageously fighting a battle for his health.
Dear Patrick: your faith in our Savior makes all
the difference in this journey. I love you so much.

to everyone fighting their own battles. Remember,
God fights our battles in a more real way than we can ask or imagine.

and to Jesus, who fought the ultimate battle on the cross
and won the war between good and evil; who is coming soon
to take us home, to a place where there are no more battles,
where there is no more suffering, no more death.

I love you, my dear Redeemer.

CONTENTS

INTRODUCTION

Battles. In this world, we all fight battles. We battle with the unexpected, with exhaustion, with anxiety, with discouragement. A battle is raging inside every person you encounter. We live in a world of sin, constantly confronting obstacles that we never planned nor expected. The battles take place in our minds as we face our foes; meet adverse circumstances; or experience complications in our families, challenges at work, or loss of health.

The Bible is a trustworthy source of guidance in times of uncertainty and confusion. In its pages, I've found great comfort in how God has always been a present help for His people in times of difficulty. In biblical times, in kingdoms or tribal societies, the people of God often faced much stronger enemies than themselves. Whether they were conquering the Promised Land or fighting for freedom, there was always something different about the people of Yahweh (Jehovah)—God was fighting for them and actively intervening on their behalf. Therefore, their battles were won in unusual and often counterintuitive ways. God was teaching them that He was in charge of their battle. The battle belongs to the Lord!

When they were no match to the opposing forces, they simply had to take their stand and watch God act. He parted the waters of the Red Sea to make a path for them to cross over. On another occasion, He created confusion among their enemies so that they turned on each other, leaving Israel without an opponent. He strengthened His people through divine intervention and enabled them to accomplish His purposes in the face of the fiercest opposition. The battles were won in supernatural ways. Furthermore, they were not just physical battles in Israel's history but also served as metaphors for salvation, teaching us that God is the only One who can do for us what we can't do for ourselves.

The conflict between good and evil started in heaven. The Bible tells us: "And there was war in heaven, Michael and his angels waging war with the dragon. The dragon and his angels waged war, and *they were not strong enough*, and there was no longer a place found for them in heaven. And the great dragon was thrown down, the serpent of old who is called the devil and Satan, who deceives the whole world; he was thrown down to the earth, and his angels were thrown down with him" (Revelation 12:7–9; emphasis added). Satan and his angels were expelled from heaven! And did you notice the highlighted sentence? The evil one and his angels *were not strong enough!* What a relief! Not strong enough to overcome our Lord! Woo-hoo and amen!

Then the adversary took it upon himself to make our lives miserable here on earth. He introduced sin, disease, and suffering, and we ended up with a sinful nature and with death never far from our door. But God intervened. Jesus, God in the flesh, came down to live a perfect life in our place. He surrendered His life on the cross as a sacrifice for our sin and was raised from the dead on the third day. This is the incredibly good news we call *the gospel*: Jesus did for us what we couldn't do for ourselves. And everyone who believes in His sacrifice has forgiveness of sins and eternal life (see John 3:16).

But you may be wondering: what does this have to do with my daily battle with cancer, addiction, financial challenges, trouble in my marriage? Oh! So glad you asked! The same God who fought in the greatest battle ever to secure your eternal salvation with His blood also fights your daily battles on your behalf right here and right now!

In this book, we will analyze twelve biblical stories about battles where God intervened supernaturally to aid His people. And we will discover that the biblical characters experienced powerlessness and struggled with discouragement, fear, lack of trust, and anxiety just like we do. And God, in His mercy, did for them what they couldn't do for themselves. I encourage you to watch the videos that accompany each chapter of this book: a TV series entitled *The Battle Is the Lord's* that is available free of charge to stream on-demand on our ministry website, Jesus101.tv. Each video discusses the content of the corresponding chapter of this book. My prayer is that you will find real encouragement in these Bible stories as they remind you that God's power, care, and peace are greater than anything you may have to face. As we begin this journey, let's proclaim together: *The battle belongs to the Lord!*

So, let's get started, shall we?

Here we go! Woo-hoo!

1

The Battle of Impossibilities

Lesson 1
Impossibilities are God's specialty, not ours.
So, take your stand and watch Him fight for you.

> *However great my troubles, they are not so great as my Father's power; however difficult may be my circumstances, yet all things around me are working together for good. He who holds up yon unpillared arch of the starry heavens can also support my soul without a single apparent prop; he who guides the stars in the well-ordered courses, even when they seem to move in hazy dances, surely he can overrule my trials in such a way that out of confusion he will bring order; and from seeming evil produce lasting good.*
> —C. H. Spurgeon, "Israel at the Red Sea"

This story takes place when the sons of Israel fled their captivity in Egypt under the command of Moses, crossed the Red Sea, and traveled through the desert toward the Promised Land. Read the full account in Exodus 14.

My heart was filled with painful questions as I entered the minister's office: *How do I keep going? Where do I go from here? Is there life after this?* Pastor Mitch was my long-time counselor, but this time I entered his office with a sense that what I had feared was imminent. *How could this be happening to me?* This was definitely not part of the plan I had for my life. In his unassuming yet unforgettable style, Pastor Mitch shared two verses that have stuck with me. He opened to Exodus 14:13, 14 and read: "Moses said to the people, 'Do not fear! Stand by and see the salvation of the LORD which He will accomplish for you today. . . . The LORD will fight for you while you keep silent.' " *Wow! Really?* I was supposed to "stand by" and "keep silent"? How could the Lord make a way for me in *this* situation?

Yet decades later, *here I am.* God specializes in making a way where there isn't one. Perhaps you are, right now, facing a no-way-out situation, a catch-22, a true impossibility. But God reminds us that the battle is His. We are His children, and He fights for us, making a way where no way is visible. I am a witness!

Impossible by design

The people of Israel were elated—just out of Egypt and on their way to the Promised Land. They had just been delivered from slavery by the blood of the Passover lamb (Exodus 12; 13), and now God was guiding them in a visible way through pillars of cloud and fire (see Exodus 13).[1] What else could they need? The most incredible dream of their freedom had just come true! . But suddenly, their elation came crashing down: God said, "Tell the sons of Israel to turn back and camp" (see Exodus 14:1, 2). And not just turn back and camp, but to camp in a dead-end place, literally trapped by the sea.

And strangely, God called this impossibility His opportunity to display His power and to show that He is the Lord, Yahweh, the God who is (verse 4; see also Exodus 3:14). He even knew what Pharaoh would think (see Exodus 14:3). I find great comfort in knowing that nothing can take God by surprise. He actually orchestrates things ahead of time so that what looks impossible and detrimental can be turned into something good and in service to His redeeming purposes.

When Pharaoh realized that, with the sons of Israel leaving, his cheap labor was gone, he decided to pursue them with his chariots and officers. The all-powerful army of Egypt was chasing the just-liberated slaves, who were trapped by the sea. But Pharaoh underestimated the fact that the Lord specializes in solving impossible situations. For a moment, though, the people of Israel forgot who their God was and became terrified of the Egyptian army.

They panicked, just as we do when facing impossibilities. In their anguish, they asked three rhetorical questions: (1) "Is it because there were no graves in Egypt that you have taken us away to die in the wilderness?" (2) "Why have you dealt with us in this way, bringing us out of Egypt?" (3) "Is this not the word that we spoke to you in Egypt, saying, 'Leave us alone that we may serve the Egyptians'?" (verses 11, 12). It's interesting, isn't it? In our powerlessness, we often choose the familiar over the healthy. They wanted to go back to Egypt, the place of enslavement. Yet, in the midst of their terror, as they didn't see any way out, Yahweh gave them, through Moses, the amazing news that *He would fight for them.*

The Lord will fight for you

Right now, it's 5:15 AM, and my husband is asleep in the other room. Recently he was brought home, having spent many days in the hospital. COVID-19 affected not only his oxygen level and lungs but also his neurological system. He needs rehabilitation in order to be able to walk again and to regain other functions lost to this virus. Over the last few days, I have been watching many sermons, reassuring me that the battle is the Lord's and that the Lord will fight for us. We are in the middle of a miracle, and I trust that God will continue to open up a way in the vast sea that lies in front of us.[2]

When confronting impossibilities, we all need to hear what the people of Israel heard as they were facing Pharaoh's army with their backs against the sea: "And Moses said to the people, '*Do not be afraid. Stand still, and see the salvation of the LORD*, which *He will accomplish for you today.* For the Egyptians whom you see today, you shall see again no more forever. *The LORD will fight for you*, and you shall hold your peace' " (verses 13, 14, NKJV; emphasis added). Wow! God was about to change their perspective; He would refocus their sight: the Egyptians, who had enslaved them, they would *see* no more. Instead, they would *see* the salvation the Lord was about to accomplish on their behalf. Oh, that our eyes and minds would stay focused on the Lord when we face impossibilities. "You will keep him in perfect peace, *whose mind is stayed* on You, because he trusts in You" (Isaiah 26:3, NKJV; emphasis added).

Then the Lord's surprising command was delivered to the sons of Israel: "Go forward!" (Exodus 14:15). Go forward? Where, exactly? God's GPS creates new paths and roads where there aren't any. And that's just what He did by creating a dry path in the middle of the water. "Then Moses stretched out his hand over the sea; and the LORD swept the sea back by a strong east wind all night and turned the sea into dry land, so the waters were divided. The sons of Israel went through the midst of the sea on the dry land, and the waters were like a wall to them on their right hand and on their left" (verses 21, 22). Aren't you thrilled that we have a God who can turn the sea into *dry land*? It was the Lord who achieved the deliverance of His people. And He still does today.

And you would think that when the Egyptians saw this marvelous miracle, they would have said: "This God has power over the sea and the wind! Let's get out of here!" But instead, they went in after them, not realizing that they were stepping into the supernatural. God gave them trouble with their chariots, and that's when even the Egyptians realized that the Lord was fighting for His people: "Let us flee from Israel, for the LORD is fighting for them against the Egyptians" (verse 25). Oh, yes! Surely, God fights on behalf of His people.

God's power to deliver
God told Moses to stretch out his hand over the sea, and the waters returned and covered the Egyptian army. "Not even one of them remained" (verse 28). The same

sea, the place of deliverance for Israel, had become the tomb for those who enslaved them. God doesn't just fight for His children—He delivers them. The conclusion of the miracle is breathtaking: "Thus the LORD saved Israel that day from the hand of the Egyptians, and Israel *saw* the Egyptians dead on the seashore. When Israel *saw* the great power which the LORD had used against the Egyptians, the people feared the LORD, and they believed in the LORD and in His servant Moses" (verses 30, 31; emphasis added). As promised, their eyes *saw* the salvation of the Lord!

And after seeing this marvelous display of God's power to deliver them, all they could do was sing! They sang one of the most amazing songs recorded in the Bible, often called "The Song of Moses and Israel," and they sang it with all their hearts. Often called "The Song of Moses and Israel," it's all about the Lord, Yahweh, and His faithfulness, might, and protection (see Exodus 15:1–18). This is a flamboyant song! And for me, the most exciting thing about it is that you and I will be joining a great chorus singing this song. At the end of the Bible, Revelation 15 depicts us all standing on the sea of glass singing the song of Moses, which has now become the Song of the Lamb (verses 2–4). The parting of the Red Sea was pointing to the salvation that Jesus, the Lamb of God, would accomplish on our behalf. It was a real, historical event that also became a metaphor for salvation.

At the cross, Jesus made a way where there was no

way. He fought on our behalf by dying in our place and delivered us from our guilt as surely as Israel crossed the Red Sea. We are on our way to the Promised Land because Jesus created a dry path in the waters of sin! Woo-hoo! As He fought for our salvation, He also fights for us in our daily battles, be they anxiety, fear, anger, hurt feelings, pain, addictions, broken relationships, health issues, or whatever challenges us and worries us. He is our assurance! The Lord fought for us and won salvation; will you trust Him with everything else as well? Take your stand, wait and see. And always remember:

Lesson 1: Impossibilities are God's specialty, not ours. So, take your stand and watch Him fight for you.

---

1. For a study on Israel's Exodus journey, see Elizabeth Talbot, *The Exodus Journey* (Nampa, ID: Pacific Press®, 2020).

2. As I write the ending of this chapter, almost four weeks have gone by, and God, in His sovereignty, has chosen to perform an amazing recovery miracle for my husband, who is now back to how he was before COVID-19. And I praise Him for it! But even if God had chosen a different outcome, I trust in His sovereignty, and I believe He makes all things work for His redeeming purposes, even when we don't understand.

2

THE BATTLE
OF UNDERSTANDING

Lesson 2
God doesn't do things our way; therefore, we won't always understand Him. Yet, He asks us to trust Him anyway.

Jericho's walls fell flat: Rahab's house was on the wall, and yet it stood unmoved; my nature is built into the wall of humanity, and yet when destruction smites the race, I shall be secure. My soul, tie the scarlet thread in the window afresh, and rest in peace.
— C. H. Spurgeon, *Morning and Evening*

This story occurs at the beginning of Israel's conquest of the Promised Land after forty years in the desert. Moses has died, and now Joshua is preparing to lead his people across the Jordan river and conquer the walled city of Jericho. Spies sent ahead to gather information meet a woman named Rahab. Read the full story in Joshua 1–6.

I couldn't understand it. *Why can't he chew and swallow his food? He was eating fine before we had to take him to the hospital.* Thoughts raced through my head as I tried to make sense of what was happening. This was definitely uncharted territory. As my husband was being treated for COVID, he suddenly stopped talking and no longer could chew or swallow nor perform other basic functions. The speech therapist explained that chewing and swallowing are really complicated functions, but all I could think of was that he had been fine a few days earlier. We consulted the hospital doctors. The first one thought that it would all come back to normal in a few weeks; the other was not so sure because there was no way of knowing how the low levels of oxygen had affected his brain. The bottom line was that we didn't know or understand a lot of things. We had to wait. Then someone posted a comment on Facebook that stuck in my mind: "God created every nerve cell in the brain." Yes! God could fix everything if He chose to do so. We don't always know the outcome on this side of eternity, but we have a God who knows and understands all that we don't. Isn't that assuring?

Are you facing a situation that you don't understand? This chapter will bring you great comfort. We may believe that God is in control, but God's ways don't always make sense to us. We are often called to follow Him by faith and not by sight. Learning to surrender to God when we don't understand is part of our journey of trust in Him. So let's get started with this incredible battle in which nothing makes sense.

Wait! Where are we going?

Joshua appointed two spies and told them: "Go, view the land, *especially Jericho*" (Joshua 2:1; emphasis added).

Wait! What? Do you really mean that the first city we will try to conquer is the fortified Jericho? The one with the really thick walls? Will that be our *first* battle in the Promised Land? Surely, all kinds of questions were racing through their minds. Yet the Bible simply says: "So they went and came into the house of a harlot whose name was Rahab, and lodged there" (verse 1). Wait! What? *A harlot?* Some early sources tried to clean it up and called Rahab an "innkeeper," but the New Testament says that she really was a harlot, or prostitute (see Hebrews 11:31).

Jericho was a city-state with its own king and army. It was located about five miles from the Jordan River. We are not told much about what the spies found out, but we know that Rahab hid them, covered them, lied for them—and then made one of the most startling and complete confessions about the God of Israel that we find in the Old Testament:

"I know that the LORD has given you the land, and that the terror of you has fallen on us, and that all the inhabitants of the land have melted away before you. For we have heard how the LORD dried up the water of the Red Sea before you when you came out of Egypt, and what you did to the two kings of the Amorites who were beyond the Jordan, to Sihon and Og, whom you utterly destroyed. When we heard it, our hearts melted and no courage remained in any man any longer because of you;

for the LORD your God, He is God in heaven above and on earth beneath" (verses 9–11).

Wow! Not only does she confess that the God of Israel is God of heaven and earth, but she also gives testimony of the marvelous deliverance and amazing victories that Yahweh has already done on behalf of Israel. And now the spies know that—no matter how thick those walls may look—the hearts of the inhabitants of the land are melting in fear.

And so sure that Yahweh will give them the city, she then makes the surprising petition that she and her whole family be spared (see verses 12, 13), a request that the spies are willing to grant: "We will deal kindly and faithfully with you" (verse 14). She was to gather her whole family inside her house that was in the wall and then tie a cord of scarlet thread in the window of her house. If she did that and didn't tell anyone about their deal, she and her family would be saved. And I love that she tied that *cord of assurance* in the window as soon as the spies were lowered from that same window (verse 21).

The scarlet cord was her assurance of survival. What is yours? Where do you find assurance when you don't understand the circumstances surrounding you? Do you rely on God's promises and His faithfulness to fulfill them? What about when you step into uncharted territory or when you go ways that you have never gone before?

You have not passed this way before

The phrase *you have not passed this way before* has become really important for me in the last few months. As a family and as a country, we are going through things that we have never experienced. Every day, we step into uncharted territory. As human beings, we've never been to the future—yet God is already there. Nothing surprises Him. Furthermore, He promises to guide us there if we let Him.

The time for Israel to cross over to the Promised Land had arrived. The Jordan River was their first obstacle. The ark of God's presence would lead the people; they were to follow it, but not too closely. And I treasure the reason God gave them: "Do not come near it, *that you may know the way by which you shall go, for you have not passed this way before*" (Joshua 3:4; emphasis added). They needed to know which way to go, and God Himself was going to lead them because they had never been *there* before. I hope this assures you as much as it does to me.

And what happened next is another one of the great miracles of Yahweh recorded in the Bible: "When those who carried the ark came into the Jordan, and the feet of the priests carrying the ark were dipped in the edge of the water . . . , the waters which were flowing down from above stood and rose up in one heap, a great distance away at Adam. . . . So the people crossed opposite Jericho. And the priests who carried the ark of the covenant of the LORD stood firm on dry ground in the middle of the Jordan while all Israel crossed on dry ground, until all the nation had finished crossing the Jordan" (verses 15–17). Wow! God has a thousand ways for us to go forward where we see only a dead end.

Next, they chose twelve men, one from each tribe, who brought up stones from the middle of the river as a memorial, a testimony for future generations (see Joshua 4:21–24) about what God did for them. How important that you record the mighty acts of God on your behalf because you will need to remember these when you go through difficult times and uncharted territory. After my husband recovered from COVID, which I believe was God's miracle, we bought a cross with an inscription: "By His stripes we are *healed*" (Isaiah 53:5, NKJV; emphasis added). We placed it on the wall in our bedroom, and every time I see it, I remember what God did on our behalf.

As with the Red Sea, Yahweh's drying up the waters of the Jordan so that Israel could cross had a very specific purpose: "That all the peoples of the earth may know that the hand of the LORD is mighty, so that you may fear the LORD your God forever" (Joshua 4:24). Oh, yes! Did I tell you? God is *always* orchestrating events for His redemptive purposes. Nothing is wasted!

Unusual instructions

And now it was time to prepare for battle. And you would think that the Israelites started talking strategy and sharpening their swords. But they did not get instructions like that. Instead, they got "unusual" instructions: Joshua was to circumcise the sons of Israel (Joshua 5:2–9). Wait. What? Now? Right before the battle?

It is beyond understanding, isn't it? Yet this would be a holy battle. All the Israelites who had been circumcised before had died in the desert (except Joshua and Caleb). And the new generation had to know that they were part of a spiritual covenant, that they belonged to the Lord. And this was way more important than having the "right" tools to fight. While camped at Gilgal and waiting for all the males to heal, they observed the Passover (verse 10), a feast of remembrance about how Yahweh had redeemed them from slavery through the blood of the lamb.

I can imagine the people feeling like they were on holy ground. And, as if the circumcision and Passover were not enough, the day after the Passover, they ate some of the produce of the land, and on the next day, the manna ceased. After forty years! Now they could eat from what the land produced. Wow! And do you have any doubt that He can provide for what you need?

After these events, when he was close to Jericho, Joshua had an unusual encounter with the Captain of the Lord's armies. When Joshua realized who the man was, he bowed down and received more unusual instructions: "Remove your sandals from your feet, for the place where you are standing is holy" (verse 15). Oh, yes! This was definitely going to be a holy battle!

Joshua then received a pre-assurance from Yahweh: "The LORD said to Joshua, 'See, I have given Jericho into your hand, with its king and the valiant warriors' " (Joshua 6:2). Don't you love it? A *pre-assurance* that God had already *given* Jericho into their hands. This is also how redemption works. We have a pre-assurance of salvation because He has already given the heavenly Promised Land to all who believe in the blood of His sacrifice on the cross. It is a gift, and it is for sure!

And then they got the most unusual instructions of all: "You shall march around the city, all the men of war circling the city once. You shall do so for six days. Also, seven priests shall carry seven trumpets of rams' horns before the ark; then on the seventh day you shall march around the city seven times, and the priests shall blow the trumpets. . . . All the people shall shout with a great shout; and the wall of the city will fall down flat." (verses 3–5). Wait! What?

This battle is the Lord's

There are times when we don't understand what is going on, and yet, we are called to do what the Lord says. And even though nothing was making much sense, Joshua and his people did as the Lord commanded them. Seven priests carried seven trumpets and, along with the men of war, went around the city for seven days. And on the seventh day, they went around seven times (see verse 4). The number seven is very important in the Bible because it reminds us that our Creator is also our Redeemer, the

One who fights our battles, and we can rest in Him, both for our eternal salvation and for our daily battles. This is why God blessed the seventh day and asked us to keep it holy: to remember who He is and who we are in Him (Genesis 2:2; Exodus 20:8–11; Deuteronomy 5:12–15).

On the seventh day, they went around the city seven times, and then the miracle occurred: "So the people shouted, and priests blew the trumpets; and when the people heard the sound of the trumpet, the people shouted with a great shout and the wall fell down flat, so that the people went up into the city, every man straight ahead, and they took the city" (Joshua 6:20). All they did was walk and shout—and the walls fell down! That is because the battle was the Lord's, and He was making things happen His way.

And what happened to Rahab? So glad you asked! "Rahab the harlot and her father's household and all she had, Joshua spared" (verse 25). Yes, the scarlet cord in the window signaled that in this house, they believed in the God of Israel. And I believe with all my heart that the red cord was a parallel symbol to the Passover lamb's blood that they had placed on their doorposts to be spared from destruction back in Egypt (see Exodus 12). Yes! Both pointed to the blood of Jesus as the only way that we will be spared when destruction comes to this world. Isn't that amazing? We are safe because we believe in His blood, and that is the one thing necessary for salvation!

Rahab became the mother of Boaz, who married Ruth, who in turn became the mother of Obed, who was the grandfather of king David. This means that Rahab, the harlot, is in the genealogy of Jesus (see Matthew 1:5). Wait! What? Yes, she is one of the great grandmothers of Jesus Christ. Doesn't that fill you with the great assurance of His grace?

The battle of Jericho reminds us of what happens when we have faith in God. "By faith the walls of Jericho fell down after they had been encircled for seven days. By faith Rahab the harlot did not perish along with those who were disobedient, after she had welcomed the spies in peace" (Hebrews 11:30, 31). Yes, all by faith . . . for they believed that the battle was the Lord's. Are you ready to believe Him, even when you don't understand everything? Remember:

Lesson 2: God doesn't do things our way; therefore, we won't always understand Him. Yet, He asks us to trust Him anyway.

3

THE BATTLE
OF REASSURANCE

Lesson 3
God's arms are long enough to save us, no matter how dark the detour we've taken.

> *I shall never meet a man who has sinned so desperately that I can say of him he never can be saved. Ah! No; that arm of mercy which was long enough to save me is long enough to save you.*
> —C. H. Spurgeon, "Manasseh"

At this point in the story of the conquest of the Promised Land, the Israelites have conquered two major cities, and several kings make an alliance to stop their advance. This results in Joshua and the Israelites having to defend a new ally against five armies at once. Read the full account in Joshua 9:1–10:15.

M any years ago, I sang in a group called Opus 7, under the direction of Ariel Quintana. We used to sing a song by Dawn Thomas Yarbrough, "His Heart Is Big Enough." The lyrics of the chorus always touch me:

His arms are long enough to save you
To give you another chance . . .
His heart is big enough to love you
So run back to Him today[1]

Isn't that reassuring? We all have been there, wondering whether God can still bless us after we took a bad detour. Perhaps you are pondering that question today. Let us continue our study of the battles in the Bible. These are metaphors of salvation that teach us that God is fighting on our behalf. We will discover that God's arms are long enough to save us, no matter how dark our detours.

When we forget

After the amazing victory in Jericho, the people of Israel became overconfident and thus experienced a terrible defeat in their fight against Ai (see Joshua 7). The human heart is deceitful; sometimes, we forget that it was the Lord who delivered us, and we start trusting in our own strength. There is no mention that they took counsel from the Lord; they sent a smaller force to fight against Ai and were defeated. "So the hearts of the people melted and became as water" (verse 5). God revealed to Joshua that Israel had transgressed His commands by keeping things that they were instructed not to take. God's being merciful doesn't mean that He ignores our concealed sin. Once Joshua dealt with the situation, God gave them victory over Ai. You would think this was the last time they forgot to ask for counsel from the Lord, but that was not the case.

"When the inhabitants of Gibeon heard what Joshua had done to Jericho and to Ai, they also acted craftily" (Joshua 9:3, 4), and they deceived Israel with worn-out sacks, clothes, and wineskins; patched sandals on their feet; and dry bread. They made it look as if they had come from very far away, from a distant country, and they asked for a covenant of peace. They related how they had heard of all the victories of Israel and were afraid. Though suspicious at first, Joshua and his people made such a covenant to let them live without realizing that they had been deceived and were actually making a covenant with their neighbors whom they were supposed to conquer. The most revealing sentence in the whole narrative is found in verse 14: "So the men of Israel took some of their provisions, and *did not ask for the counsel of the LORD*" (emphasis added).

You've got to be kidding me! How is that possible?! They forgot to ask for God's counsel again? But before we judge them too harshly, we might do well to ponder our own detours . . . At least, I can relate. God delivered me from my own foolishness many times, only for me to find myself later on in a similar spot. How about you?

When the Israelites realized what they had done, it was too late. They had already sworn to the Gibeonites by Yahweh and could not go back on their word (see verse 18). They made them servants—that is, hewers of wood and drawers of water—of the congregation. The

Gibeonites were fine with that because they got to keep their lives. But Israel's foolishness had consequences.

Will God help us with the consequences?

When King Adoni-zedek of Jerusalem heard how Israel had captured Jericho and then Ai and had made a covenant with Gibeon, "he feared greatly, because Gibeon was a great city, like one of the royal cities, and because it was greater than Ai, and all its men were mighty" (Joshua 10:2). He decided that he needed to do something about this and made an alliance with four other kings. The five of them, with their respective armies, went against Gibeon (see verses 3–5). This wasn't a weak enemy, oh no! This was a mighty alliance, and the Gibeonites called on their newly acquired ally: *Israel! Come help us!*

Oh no! Is it possible that Joshua and his men now have to fight for those who had deceived them? Have you ever found yourself in a bind that you had caused yourself? And do you ever wonder whether God would help you when it was your foolishness that got you there in the first place? Obviously, Joshua was thinking along those lines because God gave him a reassuring message. "The LORD said to Joshua, 'Do not fear them, for I have given them into your hands; not one of them shall stand before you' " (verse 8). I can't even start to imagine what this reassurance from God meant to Joshua. I am sure it reignited his confidence after his foolish diversion. God's original promise to him was still standing, even after the detours: "Every place on which the sole of your foot treads, *I have given it to you*. . . . No man will be able to stand before you all the days of your life. . . . *I will be with you; I will not fail you or forsake you*" (Joshua 1:3–5; emphasis added). God was still faithful to His promises and would aid Joshua in this military endeavor—despite it all. God has a GPS (grace positioning system) that reroutes our journey the moment that we turn back to Him, no matter how far we've strayed. Yes! His arms are long enough to save *you*!

Joshua and his people left Gilgal and went to Gibeon, marching all night, about twenty-two miles. By now, it is becoming obvious that God is in total control, and Joshua is only His agent to fulfill His purposes.

The Lord fights for His people

What follows is one of the most explicit biblical narratives about how God works behind the scenes on behalf of His people. The story alternates between God's miraculous interventions and Joshua's human efforts. Yet, in the end, God is the One who makes everything happen.

Joshua came upon them suddenly, and the Lord confounded them before Israel (Joshua 10:9, 10). Joshua pursued them, and "the LORD threw large stones from heaven . . . ; there were more who died from the hailstones than those whom the sons of Israel killed with the sword" (verse 11). Then Joshua spoke to the Lord, and God honored His request for a miracle (see verses 12, 13; you won't believe what Joshua asked for!).

The narrative continues alternating between God and Joshua. God is the One with the power, and Joshua is His agent. You see, *we are no match for the battles that we face, yet our battles are no match for the God who fights for us.*

"Then Joshua spoke to the LORD . . . ,

> 'O sun stand still at Gibeon,
> And O moon in the valley of Aijalon.'
> So the sun stood still, and the moon stopped,
> Until the nation avenged themselves of their enemies.

". . . And the sun stopped in the middle of the sky and did not hasten to go down for about a whole day" (verses 12, 13). Wait! What? Oh, yes! God's power is limitless. Even after a foolish detour, once you come back to your Maker, there is no limit on what He will do for you.

The next verse summarizes the passage: "There was no day like that before it or after it, when the LORD listened to the voice of a man; *for the LORD fought for Israel*" (verse 14, emphasis added). God fought for Israel, and He still fights for us!

Once again, we discover that the battles in the Bible are metaphors for salvation. God had made a covenant with Israel, and He has made a covenant of salvation with us. At the cross, He sealed the covenant with His blood, and when you come back to Him, you can live with full assurance, even after you have temporarily deviated from the right path. Have you taken a detour and found yourself in trouble? As the introductory song reads, "run back to Him today." You will find that He is waiting for you with open arms. When you come back to Him, your heart will experience the graceful reassurance that we all long for: "For I am convinced that neither death, nor life, nor angels, nor principalities, nor things present, nor things to come, nor power, nor height, nor depth, nor any other created thing, will be able to separate us from the love of God which is in Christ Jesus our Lord" (Romans 8:38, 39). Remember,

Lesson 3: God's arms are long enough to save us, no matter how dark the detour we have taken. So, run back to Him today.

---

1. Dawn Thomas, "His Heart Is Big Enough to Love You" (Bravo and Encore Music, 1991).

4

THE BATTLE
OF INCLUSIVITY

Lesson 4:
You have a divine calling. Arise and step into your God-given purpose, even when it doesn't conform to other people's opinions.

> *Deborah sang concerning the overthrow of Israel's enemies, and the deliverance vouchsafed to the tribes: we have a far richer theme for music; we have been delivered from worse enemies, and saved by a greater salvation. Let our gratitude be deeper; let our song be more jubilant.*
> —C. H. Spurgeon, "Songs of Deliverance"

Before the ancient nation of Israel had kings, they had judges. These leaders guided the sons of Israel by implementing the Lord's counsel. This story shows how a woman was chosen by God to lead His people to victory against a powerful enemy. Read the full story in Judges 4; 5.

Al wasn't doing great at school. So many subjects were difficult. In addition, he didn't share the sporting interests that his classmates enjoyed and so didn't fit in anywhere. His teacher told him that he would never amount to anything and advised him to drop out of school. Al took the teacher's advice and quit school. He eventually made it to a technical college where, after flunking a physics class, he barely passed his seniors' exams with one of the lowest grades in his graduating class.[1] Al's full name, by the way, was Albert Einstein. Who would have thought at the time that Al would become one of the most influential scientists of all times!

Throughout history, there have always been people who considered it their duty to tell others what they could or couldn't do. These opinions have usually originated from a particular culture or tradition or simply a sense of superiority or a need for control. Today, there is no difference. There are times when, because of our age, race, or gender, we are told that we can't do something God has called us to do. However, when it comes to our purpose in life, God breaks all the barriers and calls us to stand in the place He planned for us, even if it's not very popular. Every one of us has a role in redemption history; we all live within the much larger context of the covenant of salvation God made with the human race. When we, like Deborah, take our place that God has for us, we will find a song in our hearts—and who knows, God might make another Bible story out of our lives.

Challenging the status quo

There is nothing wrong with women in the kitchen. I delight in cooking. But this is not the *only* place for me. Deborah knew that for herself, too. When God raised judges as leaders to deliver His people (after Joshua), in spite of what the culture may have dictated, Deborah got out of her kitchen long enough to play a very important role in the history of Israel.

When God needed a strong leader, someone who would rally the military to fight their enemies, He chose . . . a woman! She was also a prophetess. God chose Deborah—the only female judge in the book of Judges. "Now Deborah, a prophetess, the wife of Lappidoth, was judging Israel at that time. She used to sit under the palm tree of Deborah between Ramah and Bethel in the hill country of Ephraim; and the sons of Israel came up to her for judgment" (Judges 4:4, 5). In a culture that did not hold women's intellects in high esteem, she became the leader of the nation. Her authority was further legitimized by her prophetic gift. Deborah was a multi-gifted and courageous woman.

She called Barak and delivered a message to him from the Lord: "Behold, the LORD, the God of Israel, has commanded, 'Go and march to Mount Tabor, and take with you ten thousand men from the sons of Naphtali and from the sons of Zebulun' " (verse 6). God is calling this tribal leader from Kedesh-Naphtali to become a national leader. But that wasn't all God said: "I will draw out to you Sisera, the commander of Jabin's army, with his chariots and his many troops to the river Kishon, and *I will give him into your hand*" (verse 7; emphasis added). Wow! This was a multiphase and detailed plan, and victory was *pre-assured*!

Barak and his men were to go to Mount Tabor. Yet God would drive Sisera and his army to the river Kishon. It seems like they are going to two different places, doesn't it? I will tell you a bit later why the geography is so important in this battle.

Then comes the shocking answer from Barak to Deborah: "If you will go with me, then I will go; but if you will not go with me, I will not go" (verse 8). Wait! What? Do you *really* want a woman to go with you into battle? What are you thinking? But Barak didn't care much about what the status quo was in his culture or that ten thousand men were with him. He wanted the security of prophetic guidance that Deborah could offer. Therefore, he asked her to join him in the battle.

You want me to do—*what?*

Has God ever surprised you by asking you to do something that you never expected? God has absolutely shocked me many times. For example, for much of my life, I was afraid of flying. It was so bad that I had to take medication to get on a plane. But then I was called to lead a media ministry, which entailed frequent plane travel. I had to settle this issue with God. I told Him that I was willing to fly anywhere to fulfill my calling but He had to take away my fear of flying so that I could do what He was calling me to do. Now, it's no longer an issue; I'm often dozing off as the plane takes off. But that wasn't the only time God shocked me. Many years earlier, I received the biggest surprise of my life when, working in the business world, I got a call to full-time ministry. But I will leave that story for another chapter. Yes, at times, God shocks and shakes us up by asking us to do something that we never expected.

Barak was willing to follow God's plan only if Deborah would go with him into battle. We don't know whether Deborah had to borrow body armor or what she did next; all we know is that when she married Lappidoth, she couldn't have imagined that one day she would be leading an army into battle. Yet she was resolved to go wherever God wanted her. "She said: 'I will surely go with you; nevertheless, the honor shall not be yours on the journey that you are about to take, for the LORD will sell Sisera into the hands of a woman.' Then Deborah arose and went with Barak to Kedesh" (verse 9). You might think that the woman who gave Sisera the death blow was Deborah, but it wasn't. It was Jael, the wife of Heber, who killed the captain of their enemies (see verse 21). Yes, another woman!

Now, back to the battle. One of the fascinating things about the geography of this battle is the way that God *preplanned* everything. If you google an image of Mount Tabor, you will see that it is quite steep. There is no way that Sisera would have attempted to climb this mountain in chariots. So, God commanded Barak and his ten thousand men to march to Mount Tabor, and God said that He would draw Sisera and his chariots to the river Kishon. And that's exactly where Sisera went. Probably there was ample space for maneuvering the chariots there. When the word came from Deborah, Barak and his men went down to the river Kishon, and God gave the enemy into their hands. Furthermore, it seems like God also sent a flood because "the torrent of Kishon swept them away" (Judges 5:21). It's encouraging to realize that God knows every detail of our circumstances. Nothing takes Him by surprise. He *preplans* the best way out. Isn't that encouraging?

When the right moment came, "Deborah said to Barak, 'Arise! For this is the day in which the LORD has given Sisera into your hands; behold, the LORD has gone out before you' " (Judges 4:14).

Remember this phrase: the Lord goes out before us and *preplans* our deliverance. This section of the story ends with Jael, Heber's wife, killing Sisera (verses 21, 22). The conclusion is summarized like this: "So God subdued on that day Jabin the king of Canaan before the sons of Israel" (verse 23). Even though He used human agents, it was God who subdued the enemy. He does the same today. Woo-hoo!

Let us celebrate!

Then comes the exuberant celebration, a duet by Deborah and Barak (see Judges 5:1). The song highlights the Lord's victory and majesty (verses 1–15). The fact that this is a *duet* reminds me of how God calls everyone, men and women, young and old, black and white. God promised this for our times through the prophet Joel:

"It will come about after this
That I will pour out My Spirit on all mankind;
And your sons and daughters will prophesy,
Your old men will dream dreams,
Your young men will see visions.
Even on the male and female servants
I will pour out My Spirit in those days" (Joel 2:28, 29).

Get ready! God calls everyone and often leads us into unexpected roles and places! As C. H. Spurgeon said, "The Lord can still use feeble instrumentalities. Why not me? He may use persons who are not commonly called to great public engagements. Why not you?"[2] This brings us back to the lesson for this chapter:

Lesson 4: You have a divine calling. Arise and step into your God-given purpose, even when it doesn't conform to other people's opinions.

And the theme of our song is the *gospel*, the good news that the final victory has already been won at the cross. Jesus is our victorious King who has already triumphed over our enemies on our behalf. He is coming soon to take over this world of sin, and there will be no more death nor pain! Oh yes! We have so much to sing about! Let's sing it all together and with all our hearts!

"Deborah sang concerning the overthrow of Israel's enemies, and the deliverance vouchsafed to the tribes: we have a far richer theme for music; we have been delivered from worse enemies, and saved by a greater salvation. Let our gratitude be deeper; let our song be more jubilant. Glory be unto God, we can say that our sins, which were like mighty hosts, have been swept away, not by that ancient river, the river Kishon, but by streams which flowed from Jesus' side."[3]

---

1. See "Albert Einstein," Character Education Lessons, http://www.character-education.info/resources/Albert_Einstein_Character.htm.

2. Charles H. Spurgeon, *Faith's Checkbook: A Treasury of Daily Devotionals by C. H. Spurgeon* (Chicago: Moody Press, 1987), June 21.

3. Charles H. Spurgeon, "Songs of Deliverance," https://www.spurgeon.org/resource-library/sermons/songs-of-deliverance/#flipbook/.

5

THE BATTLE
OF FEARFULNESS

Lesson 5
God offers us His peace to overcome our fears.
Don't let your heart be anxious, for the eternal
God fights your battles.

> *Our anxiety does not empty tomorrow of its*
> *sorrows, but only empties today of its strengths.*
> —Aleander McLoren, quoted by
> C. H. Spurgeon, *The Salt Cellars*

In the time of the judges, Israel falls under the oppression of the Midianites, and God chooses Gideon, a virtually unknown member of a lesser family, to lead three hundred men into an unusual battle against their enemy. Read the full story in Judges 6; 7.

When I was a little girl, my father was a church administrator in South America. These were difficult times of political upheaval. One day, he received an anonymous letter threatening that his only daughter, Elizabeth, would be kidnapped unless he met the demands listed in the letter. It mentioned me by name!

I remember the situation distinctly because everyone was on alert. During those difficult months, several measures were introduced to protect me. For example, I was not allowed to walk to school by myself, and no one was allowed to pick me up from school except my parents. I am told that a pastor had asked me if I had been afraid, to which I had answered: "No! Jesus takes care of me!" *Oh, the faith of a child.* (How I wish I would always answer that way.) During desperate times, fear and anxiety often sneak into our minds. And yet God offers us His peace, which is greater than all our fears.

Desperate times

These were definitely desperate times. The Midianites were disrupting Israel's life so much that "the sons of Israel made for themselves the dens which were in the mountains and the caves and the strongholds" (Judges 6:2). Israel's enemies would destroy their crops, coming in like locusts and leaving nothing behind. This was not a mere threat! It was actually happening, and God's people were afraid and anxious. We get glimpses of the extent of the problem when the Lord appears to Gideon as he is "beating out wheat in the wine press in order to save it from the Midianites" (verse 11). A wine press is for wine pressing, and yet Gideon is beating out wheat there because he is afraid and hiding. Perhaps your circumstances have corralled you, too. You are hiding, feeling trapped, barely surviving.

Then the Lord said to him: "The LORD [Yahweh] is

with you, O valiant [or mighty] warrior" (verse 12). I can imagine Gideon looking over his shoulder, thinking, *Who is He talking to? Definitely not me; I am no mighty warrior!* Then all his pent-up fears find their voice in Gideon's raw, untamed, and unadulterated perspective: "If the LORD is with us, why then has all this happened to us? And where are all His miracles which our fathers told us about, saying, 'Did not the LORD bring us up from Egypt?' But now the LORD has abandoned us and given us into the hand of Midian" (verse 13). Who cannot relate? If God is with us, why is this happening to us? Where are all the miracles of old?

"The LORD looked at him" (verse 14) and then uttered the words that would change Gideon's life and Israel's destiny: "Have I not sent you?"

From fear to peace

Who? Me? My family is the least in our tribe, and I am the youngest in my house (verse 15). *No way! I hope Yahweh finds someone else to deliver us. . . . I am not the guy.* You can see the fear raging in his mind. But what Gideon didn't know was that God usually chooses the least and the last. He typically picks the fearful and the anxious ones so that when the battle takes place, we all know that it is God's glory, not a human accomplishment, that shines through.

And to Gideon's fearful excuses, God answers: "Surely I will be with you, and you shall defeat Midian as one man" (verse 16). *Gideon, Gideon, Gideon, it's not about you but about Me!* The antidote to your fear is God's presence, not your strength or resources. How is that for great news? And God promises more than His presence to Gideon; He promises victory. The victory is pre-assured simply because of God's presence in the battle.

But Gideon, like us, is fearful. So he asks for a sign, and it won't be the last time. Besides, when he did receive the sign through the fire, which consumed his offering, he got scared because he realized that he had seen the face of the angel of the Lord (see verses 17–22). Yet Yahweh calmed his fears: " 'Peace to you, do not fear; you shall not die.' Then Gideon built an altar there to the LORD and named it The LORD is Peace [*Yahweh Shalom*]" (verses 23, 24). Yes, the Lord is our peace; and His peace overpowers our fears. And from now on, would Gideon be the most courageous man in the world because of his supernatural encounter with God? No, not really, and that is because our human hearts are frail, and we easily and quickly switch from God's peace back to our fears and insecurities. That's why we constantly need to seek God's peace so that we are not controlled by our fears.

That same night, God asked Gideon to destroy the altar of Baal that belonged to his father and to build an altar to the Lord in its place. And "Gideon took ten men of his servants and did as the LORD had spoken to him; and because he was too afraid of his father's household and the men of the city to do it by day, *he did it by night*" (verse 27; emphasis added). Oh, our fearful human heart! How feeble and wavering. And yet, God is patient with us, for He knows our weaknesses. When the men of the city found out what had happened, they wanted to kill Gideon. But his father suggested that Baal should defend himself if he was truly a god (which, of course, Baal was not). And this whole experience was only an "appetizer": for the real battle was already looming.

Are you sure about this?

"Then all the Midianites and the Amalekites and the sons of the east assembled themselves; and they crossed over and camped in the valley of Jezreel. So *the Spirit of the LORD came upon Gideon*; and he blew a trumpet, and the Abiezrites were called together to follow him" (verses 33, 34; emphasis added). This looks like a different man, doesn't it? He then sent messengers to other tribes to come and meet him for battle. The Spirit of the Lord had come upon him to empower him for this specific mission. The Spirit of God is always *the most important weapon* in our daily battles. And yet, Gideon is human, still full of fears, and we find him asking for signs—again!

I get it! I really do! If you are called by God to head a project that is impossible for you, you want to make sure that He will do what He said He would do, right? Gideon wants to be assured again. "Then Gideon said to God, 'If You will deliver Israel through me, as You have spoken . . .' " (verse 36). OK, Gideon, it's about time for you to start really trusting God's word! Baby steps—he puts a fleece of wool on the threshing floor, which is already a small victory for him because last time, he was afraid to go out in the open to the threshing floor and was threshing wheat in the wine press. He asks God that the dew may be only on the fleece but all the ground around it may be dry. And the next day, it was so. But he then had second thoughts because this could have been a natural phenomenon. So, he asks for a reverse sign, that only the fleece be dry, with dew on the ground all around it. And it was so. Quite encouraging, right? But poor Gideon, not even these signs could have prepared him for what's coming.

Then Gideon and the 32,000 men who had gathered with him camped beside the spring of Harod. They were facing an enemy 135,000 strong; Gideon's army was less than one-fourth the size of their enemy's army. In the midst of this conundrum, the word of Yahweh came to Gideon: "The people who are with you are too many for Me to give Midian into their hands, for Israel would become boastful, saying, 'My own power has delivered me' " (Judges 7:2). Wait! What? *Too many? We are not even 25 percent of the enemy's count!* No, no, no, says God. You will think you did it. And the battle is the Lord's! So, Gideon was to issue this invitation: "Whoever is afraid and trembling, let him return and depart from Mount Gilead" (verse 3). And 22,000 left. Wow! Fear is powerful, isn't it? I can't imagine what went through Gideon's mind when only 10,000 remained.

But then, God said, "They are still too many" (see verse 4). *Too many? In which universe?* God's universe. His ways are not our ways; His thoughts are not our thoughts. Then God gave them a test that involved the way they drank water (verses 4–6). How many were left after the test? Three hundred men. Wait! What?

God's miraculous intervention

Obviously, now it was impossible for Gideon and his three hundred men to win this battle. Victory could come only by God's intervention: "The LORD said to Gideon, '*I will deliver you with the 300 men* who lapped and will give the Midianites into your hands; so let all the other people go, each man to his home' " (verse 7; emphasis added). Have you ever run out of resources so completely that your solution could come only from God? When you are in such a place, the only way not to be consumed by fear is to follow where He leads.

God was ready to go into battle. But, because He knew Gideon, He said: " 'But *if you are afraid* to go down, go with Purah your servant down to the camp, and you will hear what they say; and afterward your hands will be strengthened that you may go down against the camp.' *So he went . . .*" (verses 10, 11; emphasis added).

Gideon is still afraid! *So he went with his servant.* And at the camp, he heard one of his enemies relating his dream to a friend, and the friend replied, "This is nothing less than the sword of Gideon the son of Joash, a man of Israel; God has given Midian and all the camp into his hand" (verse 14). When Gideon heard this, "he bowed in worship. He returned to the camp of Israel and said, 'Arise, for the LORD has given the camp of Midian into your hands'" (verse 15). Finally, after the fourth sign, he is convinced. God's peace, His *shalom*, is overpowering his fearful heart. How many signs does it take for God's perfect and loving plan to cast away our fears? That's how feeble our hearts are.

Gideon, now ready, divided the three hundred men into three companies. They took trumpets and torches inside pitchers. They came to the enemy camp at night and "blew the trumpets and smashed the pitchers" (verse 19) and cried, "A sword for the LORD and for Gideon!" (verse 20). "When they blew 300 trumpets, the LORD set the sword of one against another" (verse 22), and the enemy army started fighting against themselves. The men from Nephtali, Asher, and all Manasseh were called to help pursue the Midianites, and they had a decisive victory. But only because the Lord acted on their behalf.

I believe that the biggest battle took place in Gideon's mind well ahead of the actual battle on the field. He had to surrender his fears to the Lord before the victory was won. This battle was not won by Gideon's strength or the size of his army. It was won by God's presence with them. Are you waging the same battle of fearfulness? Fear is powerful, but God's peaceful presence with us is even more powerful! When we feel fearful, let's remember:

Lesson 5: God offers us His peace to overcome our fears. Don't let your heart be anxious, for the eternal God fights your battles.

This battle of Midian later on in the Bible is used as a metaphor for salvation, meaning that God achieves our salvation in much the same way He won the battle for Gideon and His men. It's all about Him!

> For You shall break the yoke of their burden and the staff on their shoulders,
> The rod of their oppressor, *as at the battle of Midian*. . . .
> For a child will be born to us, a son will be given to us;
> And the government will rest on His shoulders;
> And His name will be called Wonderful Counselor, Mighty God,
> Eternal Father, *Prince of Peace* (Isaiah 9:4–7; emphasis added).

The Prince of Peace won the battle at the cross and paid the highest price for our peace; for "the punishment that brought us *peace* was upon Him" (Isaiah 53:5, NIV; emphasis added). When it comes to our eternal salvation, many feel fearful, especially when they realize that we don't qualify: we don't have what it takes to be victorious in the battle against evil. But I have the best news for you: Jesus already won the battle on our behalf. His blood is more than sufficient to wash away your sins and your fears!

6

THE BATTLE
OF COMPARISON

Lesson 6
God fights on our behalf. Therefore, measure
the size of your giants in reference to your
mighty God and not to your own feeble human
strength.

> *If you see before you a work by means of which
> you can glorify God and bless the church, do not
> hesitate, but enter upon it in reliance upon your
> God. Do not stand stuttering and stammering and
> talking about qualifications, and so on, but what
> your hand findeth to do, do it in the name of the
> Lord Jesus, who has bought you with his blood.*
> —C. H. Spurgeon,
> "The Lion-Slayer—The Giant Killer"

This story brings out the spiritual lessons of one of the Bible's best-known stories—the fateful encounter of the Philistine giant, Goliath, and a young shepherd boy who would be king, David. Read the full account in 1 Samuel 17.

My mom and I went for a ride. At that time, it was acceptable to leave a child in the car while running a short errand. She had opened the window a bit, and I happily sat in the car with my children's magazines. I had heard of a mysterious group of people who lived in that town. They dressed differently than we did, and I feared them. I determined to be on the lookout. Shortly after my mother was out of my sight, a girl my age, clearly belonging to the feared group, approached me and started to talk through the car window, assertively ordering me to give her my magazines, which I refused to do. She then responded with one of the most terrifying threats I had ever heard: "I will call my mom, and you'll see what she will do!" I imagined a giant woman coming to the car, forcing the door open, and taking me away forever. Though a product of my own imagination, these thoughts were real to me. What could I do? I was no match for a giant. The adrenaline started flowing through my little body, and I managed to slide through the small opening in the window and leave the car, screaming at the top of my lungs. I thought that I was in danger, and anything was better than staying in the car. I started walking down the street, crying so loud that my mother came running out. Between sobs, I tried to explain to her that a giant woman was about to kidnap me. Of course, we never saw the giant woman, but she was definitely real to me! My mother was never able to figure out how I could have slid through the small opening in the window.

Scary giants

Whether real or imagined, giants are scary, especially because we regularly compare their size and strength with our own. Whatever our giant—sin, sickness, sudden bad news, or some adverse circumstances—we always come up short when comparing ourselves with them. And this is what was happening to Israel.

The Philistines had gathered for battle at Socoh, in

Judah, and Saul and the men of Israel camped in the valley of Elah (see 1 Samuel 17:1, 2). The Philistines sent a *representative, or mediator*, often translated as "champion," named Goliath, from Gath. He was a real giant (about 9½ feet tall), not an imaginary one as in my childhood story. For forty days, this enemy had taunted the armies of the living God. How long has your giant been bothering you? Forty days, forty months, forty years?

King Saul was one head taller than anyone else, so, in a way, he was Israel's giant. Yet he was as terrified as his people were (see verse 11). He wouldn't fight Goliath. He was comparing the giant with himself, and of course—he didn't measure up. You know what I am talking about: the battle of comparison that takes place in our minds.

Everyone is focusing on the Philistine champion—his size, sword, helmet, javelin, the weight of his armor, and so on (see verses 4–7). Had everyone forgotten God's covenantal promises: "When you go out to battle against your enemies and see horses and chariots and people more numerous than you, do not be afraid of them; for the LORD your God, who brought you up from the land of Egypt, is with you. . . . Do not be fainthearted. Do not be afraid, or panic, or tremble before them, for the LORD your God is the one who goes with you, to fight for you against your enemies, to save you" (Deuteronomy 20:1–4)? This promise is for us as well. When we face scary giants, we often forget that these are giants only when compared to us. But compared to our mighty God, they are nothing to be fearful of.

Let us talk about God

The young David, recently anointed to be the future king of Israel, came to the battlefield, bringing supplies to his brothers. That's when he first heard the giant speaking. And we realize that David showed up talking about how big his God was, not about the size of the giant: "Who is this uncircumcised Philistine, that he should taunt the armies of the living God?" (1 Samuel 17:26). His courageous words caught the attention of the people around him. Saul sent for him, and David greeted the king with words that he had not heard in at least forty days: "Let no man's heart fail on account of him; *your servant will go and fight with this Philistine*" (verse 32; emphasis added). You would think that Saul rejoiced to hear a resolute statement like that for a change, but he responded with "You are not able . . ." (verse 33).

The lesson here? If we want to be used by God, we have to learn to ignore the many voices that will say things contrary to what God tells us. David had to ignore his brothers' opposing voices, the king's disheartening words, and surely the voices in his own head too. He had to settle the battle of comparison in his own mind before he could face the giant. The same goes for us. Once we are convinced that the Lord fights our battles, we face our giants with a completely different mindset. It's not about our strength but about His!

David went on to recall how God had delivered him from his "giants" in the past: "The LORD (Yahweh) who delivered me from the paw of the lion and from the paw of the bear, He will deliver me from the hand of this Philistine" (verse 37). He was sure that God would deliver him again. He had the assurance of God's presence. Perhaps this is one reason why God referred to David as "a man after My heart" (Acts 13:22).[1]

Even though Saul eventually said "Go!" he still kept comparing the young man in front of him with the giant. That's why he tried to clothe David in his own armor, which, of course, didn't fit. Comparing ourselves to others or comparing ourselves to the obstacles in front of us is a futile task. When I try to face my own obstacles, I come up short and get anxious. I need to take refuge in a mighty God whose strength and power are limitless. And that's what David did. He was not going to confront the giant with his own strength. Oh, no! He was coming in the name of his God!

The Lord of hosts

I visited the Valley of Elah, where David fought with Goliath. There is still a dry river bed there, and it felt very special to pick up some stones as David did. As I looked at those small stones, I pondered how God uses the most ordinary things to achieve His purposes.

David took five smooth stones and his sling (1 Samuel 17:40) and approached the Philistine champion. Goliath cursed him by his gods, to which David replied: "You come to me with a sword, a spear, and a javelin, *but* I come to you in the name of the LORD of hosts (*Yahweh Tsebaoth*), the God of the armies of Israel, whom you have taunted" (verse 45; emphasis added). David did not compare the giant with himself; instead, he declared that the giant was to fight against David's God. David was coming to the fight not in his name or power but in the name and the power of the Lord of the armies! Then David uttered a prophecy: "This day the LORD *will deliver you up into my hands.* . . . [Then] all the earth may know that there is a God in Israel, and that all this assembly may know that the LORD does not deliver by sword or by spear: for *the battle is the Lord's* and *He will give you into our hands*" (verses 46, 47; emphasis added). This is the theme of the book you are holding in your hands: *The battle is the Lord's.* And David was assured of that!

David's zeal was for the reputation of the God of Israel, not his own. We can see his passion at the end of verse 48: "David ran quickly toward the battle line to meet the Philistine" (verse 48). Oh, how I wish that we would always confront our giants with the assurance that the Lord of hosts is fighting our battles! With his sling and a stone, David defeated the giant (verses 50, 51). God uses the most ordinary agents and instruments to achieve His purposes. Saul's army pursued the Philistines, and they had a great victory that day. All because one young boy decided to talk to his giant about the size of his God. What battle are you facing today? Are you ready to tell your adversary, whoever or whatever it may be, about the awesomeness of your God? When facing giants, always remember this:

Lesson 6: God fights on our behalf. Therefore, measure the size of your giants in reference to your mighty God and not to your own feeble human strength.

The Representative

It was common in that culture to go into battle through *a representative*. But it is even more important for us to understand that principle when it comes to our spiritual life. This is the reason we can live with the assurance of salvation: our Representative, Jesus, the Descendant of David, has fought and won on our behalf (see Romans 5:18, 19). This is the good news of the gospel of Jesus Christ: we have eternal salvation not through our own power or ability but because Jesus fought in our place and won. Woo-hoo! And whenever your sins seem to be overpowering you, remember that there is a Giant fighting on your side.

"Let not your sense of sin make you think little of my Master. You are a great sinner, but he is a greater Saviour. Do not say that you have matched Christ, or overmatched him. Come, Goliath sinner, the Son of David can conquer thee or save thee yet: 'Though your sins be as scarlet, they shall be as white as snow; though they be red like crimson, they shall be as wool.' "

—C. H. Spurgeon, "The Way"

---

1. For a study of the life of David, see Elizabeth Talbot, *After God's Heart* (Nampa, ID: Pacific Press®, 2017).

7

THE BATTLE
OF EXHAUSTION

Lesson 7

God has already secured the victory for us who are weak and exhausted. So, when you are weary, go to Him. He will give you true rest.

When you are so weak that you cannot do much more than cry, you coin diamonds with both your eyes. The sweetest prayers God ever hears are the groans and sighs of those who have no hope in anything but his love.

—C. H. Spurgeon, "The Cast-off Girdle"

Before he became king, David led a band of several hundred men and temporarily lived among Israel's enemies in Ziklag. When the Amalekites raided their camp and took their families, David and his men pursued the attackers. Read the full story in 1 Samuel 30

Have you ever been at the end of your rope and had nothing left but tears? I have. It was a few weeks before my PhD dissertation defense in the United Kingdom, but I was still in the USA. The following day, I was planning to fly to Alaska for a weeklong ministerial assignment, during which time I had to make final edits to my thesis. This was the last week before the deadline. My supervisor had mailed me the manuscript with his final comments, and they were to arrive the day before my flight. This was my last chance. No more time, no more extensions. This was it. I waited and waited for the delivery, but the bell never rang. Getting a bit anxious, I opened the front door, and that's when I saw it: a note! The mailman had left a paper on my door, letting me know that the precious package with my professor's notes would be waiting for me at the central post office. *No! Not possible. You don't understand. I won't be here tomorrow!*

I frantically called the number on the note and was notified that the central office would be closing in twenty minutes. This was my last chance. I had no other options. If someone could please wait for me, they would save me eight years of my life. The person at the other end of the line was rather stoic and simply said that I should hurry. But there was no way I could make it on time. Driving like a maniac, I arrived at the central office to see everything closed and dark. I distinctly remember my desperation and exhaustion. I started knocking at the closed glass door, hoping against all hope, tears rolling down my cheeks. *This was it!* I was losing eight years of my life and thousands upon thousands of dollars. Right there, all my efforts of countless days and nights researching and writing were going down the drain. I don't know how long I knocked. Someone, please help! Then I noticed a silhouette of a person coming toward the glass door with a package in hand. And my tears of exhaustion turned into the utmost joy.

Are you exhausted, needing Someone to intervene on your behalf? Are you tired of trying, fighting, putting your best foot forward, and still feeling you are not good enough? Are you plain tired, weary, and exhausted? Then this chapter is for you.

The bad news first

David was in a bad place. Having been persecuted by the jealous King Saul, he decided to live in the Philistine country, in Gath—the very town of Goliath, the giant. He spent sixteen months living in enemy territory. No psalm was written by him during this time, as if he had lost his praise voice. He had become a double-faced man, pretending to be allied with the enemy while still an Israelite at heart. He raided the Philistine towns, killing everyone so that no one could tell the story of bloodshed and betrayal in the wake of his pursuits. He had become an impostor, bringing carnage wherever he went (see 1 Samuel 27).

Achish, king of Gath, gave David and his men the town of Ziklag to live in with their families. One day, after an interesting exchange between David and Achish (see 1 Samuel 29), David and his men returned to Ziklag—only to find it had been raided and burned down by the Amalekites. The raiders had taken all the women and children hostage (see 1 Samuel 30:1–3). "Then David and the people who were with him lifted their voices and wept until there was no strength in them to weep" (verse 4). Can you relate? Weeping until there is no strength in you anymore?

And just when you think that this downward spiraling can't get any worse, David's men started talking about stoning him. His men were not only tired but also distressed by the loss of their wives and children. So, they turned against David (see verse 6). The loss is too great, their souls too exhausted. Having taken a huge detour for the last sixteen months, what will David, the man after God's own heart, do under pressure—alone, distressed and powerless? Where will he find spiritual and emotional medicine for his broken heart? Where will he find strength for his exhausted soul?

Hitting bottom and looking up

Sometimes we fall so low that the only way left is up. Have you ever "hit bottom" and found the Lord there? That is what happened to David. After months in enemy territory, after lies and bloodshed, after his town is burned down and his wives taken captive, after his men are ready to stone him, we get a pivotal word—*but*: "*But* David strengthened himself in the LORD his God" (verse 6). In that desperate and crucial moment, David found strength in nothing else but his God. God was all he had left. When all you have left is God, that's when you discover that God is more than enough. David remembered *whose he was*! He asked the priest to bring the ephod, which was attached to the breastplate that contained the Urim and Thummim, a divinely appointed way of communication between God and His people (see Exodus 28:30; Numbers 27:21). He inquired of the Lord: " 'Shall I pursue this band? Shall I overtake them?' And He [the LORD] said to him, 'Pursue, for you will surely overtake them, and you will surely rescue all.' So David went" (1 Samuel 30:8, 9).

God gave him a pre-assurance of victory. And though we don't have an ephod with a Urim and Thummim, I believe that, as children of God, we all have the assurance that, when we are following God's revealed word, the outcome is in His hands, whether or not we understand His purposes.

Back to David. He was ready to go. "David went, he and the six hundred men who were with him, and came to the brook Besor" (verse 9). They were ready to pursue the enemy and get their families back, yet some of his men were too exhausted to go on.

Good news for the exhausted

"But David pursued, he and four hundred men, for *two hundred who were too exhausted* to cross the brook Besor remained behind " (verse 10; emphasis added). Wait! What? How exhausted do you have to be to give up on searching for your own family? Two hundred of David's men cannot cross the brook? The brook Besor had a steep side, about three hundred to four hundred feet high—quite a climb when physically and emotionally exhausted. So, one-third of his men gave up the hunt for their families. At one time or another, we, too, face exhaustion. Perhaps we can't bring ourselves to change one more diaper, or we lack the energy to prepare a complicated meal for the aging person under our care. We are just too exhausted to go on, and we don't need our inner voice telling us how terrible we are.

David continued with the four hundred men and recovered all the families and brought back a great spoil (see verses 18–20). When they came back to the brook, the two hundred men who had been left behind went out excitedly to greet them, but some of David's men were not happy to share the spoil with them: "Then all the wicked and worthless men among those who went with David said, 'Because they did not go with us, we will not give them any of the spoil that we have recovered, except to every man his wife and his children, that they may lead them away and depart' " (verse 22).

Some men were selfish and arrogant, thinking that it had been *their* strength that had achieved such a decisive victory. But then David spoke up and uttered words that reflect God's own heart: "Then David said, 'You must not do so, my brothers, with what *the LORD has given us, who has kept us and delivered into our hand the band that came against us*' " (verse 23; emphasis added). In other words, *the battle is the Lord's*! It wasn't our strength or stamina that prevailed; it was the Lord who gave us this victory. And David then created a statute and an ordinance: "For as his share is who goes down to the battle, so shall his share be who stays by the baggage; they shall share alike" (verse 24; see also verse 25). And not only did David share the spoils with the exhausted ones who had stayed behind, but he also sent some of the spoils to the elders of Judah, saying: "Behold, a gift for you from the spoil of the enemies of the LORD" (verse 26). Wow! What a celebration of God's victory! Everyone celebrated—the strong, the weak, the exhausted, and even the ones who hadn't been there.

The battle belongs to the Lord

The reason this battle is good news for the exhausted is that this principle also applies to our salvation—the reward is a gift from God; we don't earn it. None of us *deserve* salvation, no matter what we have or have not done. Jesus died for us and, in doing so, won the victory for all who choose Him. And He shares the results of His victory with all of us who are too handicapped and exhausted to be able to run the perfect race that would qualify us for eternal life.

Have you been trying so hard to gain God's approval that you end up falling flat on your face, feeling weak and burdened? Jesus has a compassionate invitation for you: "Come to Me, all who are weary and heavy-laden, and I will give you rest. Take my yoke upon you . . . , and you will find rest for your souls" (Matthew 11:28, 29). Jesus won the victory on your behalf already. So, go ahead; accept His invitation. Breathe! Rest! And remember:

Lesson 7: God has already secured the victory for us who are weak and exhausted. So, when you are weary, go to Him. He will give you true rest.

8

THE BATTLE OF PERCEPTION

Lesson 8
God's reality is experienced by faith, not by sight. Be assured of the heavenly armies that surround you at all times, even though you cannot see them.

> *I pray that the eyes of every Christian person here may be so opened that they shall never doubt that the powers on the side of truth and righteousness and God are, after all, mightier than the hosts of evil. . . . If you commit yourself to the keeping of the hand which was pierced with the nails, heaven and earth may pass away, but the Lord can never desert you.*
>
> —C. H. Spurgeon,
> "Young Man! A Prayer for You"

The prophet Elisha lived in a time marked by wonderful miracles and mortal dangers for a spiritual leader. This story shows a pagan king scheming against God's people and how God reveals His formidable presence to an anxious man. Read the story in 2 Kings 6:8–23.

When pursuing my PhD, I did not take student loans but worked full time, saving all that I could. Also, my parents were trying hard to make ends meet as they had recently retired and moved to California and were adjusting to their new budget. My birthday was coming, and we made plans to meet at a restaurant to celebrate. I was so happy! I had told my mom not to worry about getting me a gift and that if she wanted to get me something, she could go to a 99 cents store and buy some cute accessories and pins for my hair, but nothing more. I still remember the location of the restaurant, even though it was many years ago. My mom gave me a gift bag filled with colorful hair accessories, as I had asked. She had done exactly as I told her, and I was sure of the content of that gift bag. I took out the hairpins, one by one, celebrating the colors and styles. When I got to the bottom of the bag, I was surprised to find a little wooden box with beautiful hand-painted flowers on the top. She told me excitedly that she had painted it especially for me. I picked it up carefully, admiring her artistic work, but when I opened the little box—my heart almost stopped. Inside it was a tightly wrapped roll of ten one-hundred-dollar bills. One thousand dollars!

Tears flowed freely. This was exactly what I needed at that moment to pay my tuition. I hugged my parents in overflowing gratitude. Their sacrificial love, once again, had left me speechless (which is hard to do). I had been so sure that I knew the content of that gift bag, and yet I was wrong. I couldn't have imagined ahead of time what my parents were willing to do for me. Perception is our interpretation of reality, and yet, things are not always what they appear to be. Sometimes, they are much better.

Things are not always what they appear

The prophet Elisha had succeeded Elijah, who had been taken to heaven in a chariot of fire (see 2 Kings 2:11). Since that time, God had performed many miracles through the prophet Elisha. Many vessels were filled with oil so that a widow could pay her debt; the son of a Shunammite woman was raised to life; Naaman was healed from leprosy; an axe was made to float; twenty loaves of barley bread were multiplied, enough for one hundred men to eat (with plenty of leftovers). So, by the time we get to 2 Kings 6, Elisha is a well established prophet in Israel.

The king of Aram was warring against Israel, and every time he had a plan to take Israel by surprise, Elisha would warn the king of Israel ahead of time. This happened "more than once or twice" (verse 10). The king of Aram was so frustrated about this that one day he confronted his men, thinking that there was a mole in his ranks: "Will you not tell me which of us is for the king of Israel?" (verse 11). He couldn't understand why his plans never succeeded. Then, one of his servants gave him the reason: "No, my lord, O king; but Elisha, the prophet who is in Israel, tells the king of Israel the words that you speak in your bedroom" (verse 12). *That's why.* So, the king of Aram decided to take the prophet captive. When he found out that Elisha was in Dothan, "he sent horses and chariots and a great army there, and they came by night and surrounded the city" (verse 14), which raises an obvious question regarding the prophetic gift. If Elisha always knew when Aram was coming against Israel, wouldn't he also know when the army was coming after him? Of course! But Elisha's assistant didn't have the prophetic gift and almost had a heart attack the next morning.

"Now when the attendant of the man of God had risen early and gone out, behold, an army with horses and chariots was circling the city. And his servant said to him, 'Alas, my master! What shall we do?' " (verse 15), which sounds like a reasonable question. He sounds desperate, doesn't he? The attendant's perception was true: they were surrounded by a great enemy army. You know the feeling: the creditors are after you, your marriage is failing, your kid is in free fall, and everything seems to be going down the drain. You are surrounded, and the question rises in your soul: "What shall we do?" Anxiety sets in, and peace dissipates as there seems to be no light at the end of the tunnel.

And that's when the prophet tells his assistant that things aren't always what they appear: "Do not fear, for those who are with us are more than those who are with them" (verse 16). Wait! What?

What you see is not what you get

Do not fear? Why not? Aren't we in obvious trouble? Plus, the assurance that the prophet gives his assistant seems to have some flawed mathematics. What do you mean that those who are with us are more than those who are with them? Let me count how many we have on our side. One, two . . . Let's do it again: One, two. That's it! How can we possibly be more than the vast army surrounding us? You must know that feeling: when you are counting, and you get to only two: two hundred dollars left in the bank account, two more days before you are laid off, two more months to live according to the lab report, two slices of bread left in the refrigerator. Not enough. Not what we had hoped for. Our perception is what we see. And we can't see more than two. And yet the Bible reminds us over and over again: Do not fear, do not fear. The most repeated divine exhortation.

And that's when the prophet reminds his attendant, and us, that what you see is not what you get. There is much more than what we can see or perceive with our human senses. Elisha prays for a momentary bridge from our physical reality to the *unseen certainties of faith*; a prayer for a heavenly perspective, a prayer for real sight. "Then Elisha prayed and said, 'O LORD, I pray, open his eyes that he may see.' And the LORD opened the servant's eyes and he saw; and behold, the mountain was *full of horses and chariots of fire all around Elisha*" (verse 17; emphasis added). What an amazing sight, to be able to see God's reality! We better start practicing believing in these divine realities because they are more certain than what we can see with our physical eyes. The battle of perception is this: which reality will you trust? The reality you see, or the one that God says is there, even if you can't see it? The divine reality is the one you are invited to believe.

One night when I was a child, my mom and I had to walk through a dangerous neighborhood at night. She was trying to find a way home. I remember the unending industrial blocks without residences or light. And I also remember distinctively the verse my mother said we should repeat aloud over and over again: "The angel of the LORD encamps around those who fear Him, and rescues them" (Psalm 34:7).

I believe this reality with all my heart. I am never alone. No matter how dark the situation, the mountains are full of chariots of fire all around me. I invite you to believe this reality as well.

Having prayed that his servant's eyes would be opened, Elisha prayed that the eyes of their enemies would be closed. When the enemy soldiers became blind, Elisha took them to Samaria, and there he prayed that God would restore their sight. The whole army found themselves captive in the middle of the capital city of the northern kingdom. But instead of allowing the king of Israel to kill them, Elisha told the king: " 'Set bread and water before them, that they may eat and drink and go to their master.' So he prepared a great feast for them; and when they had eaten and drunk he sent them away, and they went to their master. And the marauding bands of Arameans did not come again into the land of Israel" (2 Kings 6:22, 23). They didn't get what they expected either. They got a great feast instead of the sword, which, by the way, is how God treats us.

Put your glasses on!

The battle of perception rages on in our minds. Are we going to trust what we see or what God has promised? The question applies to both our daily battles and our salvation—salvation by grace through faith. We will never see ourselves worthy of being saved, yet, we are invited to believe. Salvation is the reality that God promised to us through the sacrifice of His Son Jesus on the cross. When we put those "faith glasses" on, we receive the assurance that we are saved, not because of our entitlement, perfection, or merit but because we accept what He did for us.

The name of Jesus is very similar to the name Elisha. Elisha means "God saves," and Jesus means "Yahweh saves." Both remind us that salvation comes from God and not from us. And our daily struggles work the same way as our salvation—God fights our battles. May you come to see with the eyes of faith "the *assurance* of things hoped for, the *conviction* of things *not seen*" (Hebrews 11:1; emphasis added).

Next time your perception tells you that you are on your own, remember:

Lesson 8: God's realities are experienced by faith, not by sight. Be assured of the heavenly armies that surround you at all times, even though you cannot see them.

9

THE BATTLE
OF POWERLESSNESS

Lesson 9
Frequently, we face situations in which our strength and wisdom are not enough. Yet, we have this assurance to rely on: though we are "power-less," our God is "power-full."

The fact was the case was so altogether hopeless as far as they were concerned, that it was no use looking to anything beneath the skies, and as they were driven from all manifest earthly resorts they were compelled to lift up their eyes to God. . . . God's people resorted only to the arm invisible—the arm omnipotent—and they did well and wisely.
—C. H. Spurgeon, "The Singing Army"

After the reigns of David and Solomon his son, Israel was split into the northern (Israel) and the southern (Judah) kingdoms. One of the kings of Judah, Jehoshaphat, faced the allied armies of several enemies. Read about his response to overwhelming odds in 2 Chronicles 20:1–30.

As I greeted the new year on January 1, 2020, I had no idea what was in store for us during the following two years or how powerless I would feel. In January, I was flying to the Philippines to speak for a week of prayer at the Adventist International Institute of Advanced Studies. The day before the meetings were to start, a nearby volcano erupted unexpectedly; I entered one of the strangest weeks of my life. Everything got canceled except the week of prayer, which I had entitled "Blessed Assurance" (how fitting). It was the first time that I was preaching to a masked audience (due to the dangerous volcanic ash in the air). All of us were feeling powerless as the eruptions increased in intensity. We placed our lives in the hands of God and submitted to His will. Once the meetings were over, I flew back to the United States only to learn of a *possible* pandemic threatening the world. We did not know much about COVID-19 yet except that it was a very contagious and deadly virus. During the next two years, everyone wore masks, while feeling powerless over an invisible enemy claiming hundreds and thousands of lives every day. Once again, there were no earthly answers. All we could do was place our lives in the hands of our Creator-Redeemer. Fast-forward to January 2022. My husband was hospitalized with severe COVID-19 pneumonia. His neurological system was affected to the point where he stopped walking, talking, and swallowing. I spent every day with him at the hospital while his life hung in the balance between life and death. Science couldn't tell us whether he would ever recover what he had lost. We were powerless. All we could do was place ourselves in the hands of God.

So, what do we do when we are powerless and don't know what to do? I want to share a biblical story that helps me every time I feel powerless.

When we don't know what to do

Jehoshaphat, king of Judah, was powerless over the situation he was facing. But let me back up and tell you a few things that preceded that eventful day. In his reign, Jehoshaphat did what was right in the eyes of God (see 2 Chronicles 17:3–6). Though having made several mistakes (such as an alliance with Ahab, king of Israel), throughout his rule, he fought idolatry, and God prospered him. He possessed an impressive military force, but one day, he faced a crisis much greater than his resources and that's where we pick up the story.

"Now it came about after this that the sons of Moab and the sons of Ammon, together with some of the Meunites, came to make war against Jehoshaphat. Then some came and reported to Jehoshaphat, saying, 'A great multitude is coming against you from beyond the sea, out of Aram and behold, they are in Hazazon-tamar (that is Engedi).' Jehoshaphat was afraid" (2 Chronicles 20:1–3). This was a *great multitude*, greater than Jehoshaphat's military force. This was a foe that he couldn't face with the resources at hand. And they had already crossed the sea and were in Engedi, which is quite close to Jerusalem. No wonder the king was afraid. Perhaps today you are facing a multitude of circumstances that exceed your resources, strength, and wisdom. If so, keep reading. I believe you will find what you are looking for.

Jehoshaphat, who had learned from his past futile attempts at increasing his strength through unwise alliances, humbled himself and sought the Lord. I am so glad that verse 3 does not stop with the sentence about the king's fear but continues to reveal where he turned for help. "Jehoshaphat was afraid *and turned his attention to seek the LORD*, and proclaimed a fast throughout all Judah. So Judah gathered together to seek help from the LORD; they even came from all the cities of Judah to seek the LORD" (verses 3, 4; emphasis added). Can you imagine the whole southern kingdom of Judah gathering in Jerusalem, fasting in order to petition help from God? When we are powerless over a loved one's failing health, or over devastating financial trouble, or over a life-long relationship in peril—everything else stops, and we concentrate only on that one overpowering battle. The way Jehoshaphat and his people acted in this crisis becomes a model for all of us who face overwhelming circumstances.

A model prayer for the powerless

"Then Jehoshaphat stood in the assembly of Judah and Jerusalem, in the house of the LORD before the new court" (verse 5). What a great place for a godly leader to be. Leading his people in prayer, seeking help from the Lord. Without God, their case was hopeless. Commenting on this story, Spurgeon says (see our introductory paragraph), "the fact was the case was so altogether hopeless as far as they were concerned, that it was no use looking to anything beneath the skies." God was their only way out. Therefore, the king prayed. Five sections in this prayer are extremely helpful to follow when we face our own *great multitude.*

First, focus on *God's power*: "O LORD, the God of our fathers, are You not God in the heavens? And are You not ruler over all the kingdoms of the nations? Power and might are in Your hand so that no one can stand against You" (2 Chronicles. 20:6). That's where we start. Focusing on who He is and His might. We are powerless, but He is power-full.

Second, remember *God's past acts*: "Did You not, O our God, drive out the inhabitants of this land before Your people Israel and give it to the descendants of Abraham Your friend forever?" (verse 7). Remembering what God has done in the past, both in our lives and in redemption history, strengthens our assurance that He will act on our behalf in the future.

Third, King Jehoshaphat claimed *God's promises*: "They [the descendants of Abraham] have lived in it [this land], and have built You a sanctuary there for Your name, saying, 'Should evil come upon us, the sword, or judgment, or pestilence, or famine, we will stand before this house and before You (for Your name is in this house) and cry to You in our distress, and You will hear and deliver us' " (verses 8, 9). God is faithful to His promises. He always answers, though it might not be in the way that we were expecting. And His timing is always right, neither early nor late.

Fourth, *tell God your problem* in detail. This is not to *inform* God about what's happening (He already knows) but to place yourself in His hands in this situation. "Now behold, the sons of Ammon and Moab and Mount Seir, whom You did not let Israel invade when they came out of the land of Egypt (they turned aside from them and did not destroy them), see how they are rewarding us by coming to drive us out from Your possession which You have given us as an inheritance" (verses 10, 11). I love how specific the king gets. The Israelites, on their way to the Promised Land, had spared these people, who were now coming against them, because God had told them to. "See how they are rewarding us." It was unfair, it was a betrayal, and the king was still powerless against them. Are you in the same situation? Victim of an unfair betrayal? Tell God about it. He will fight on your behalf.

Last, *make your requests to God*, recognizing your powerlessness. "O our God, will You not judge them? For *we are powerless* before this great multitude who are coming against us; *nor do we know what to do, but our eyes are on You*" (verse 12; emphasis added). These three sentences have become a prayerful motto when I face a crisis: (1) I am powerless over this, (2) I don't know what to do, and (3) my eyes are on You. It is so true! His power is made perfect in our weakness (see 2 Corinthians 12:9).

The response of our "power-full" God
The Spirit of the Lord came upon Jahaziel, who was in the midst of the assembly (see verse 14). In this case, the response was immediate; however, sometimes, it's

a process. I have experienced situations in which I felt powerless—*for years.* All I know is that God always hears, always answers, always intervenes. Sometimes, He works the way He did this time; other times, He gives us a different perspective or removes us from the situation. Sometimes, He provides supernatural strength and patience.

The next few verses are highlighted and underlined in my Bible. Jahaziel brought a message from the Lord: "Do not fear or be dismayed because of this great multitude, *for the battle is not yours but God's." "You need not fight in this battle*; station yourselves, *stand and see the salvation of the LORD on your behalf. . . . Do not fear or be dismayed*; tomorrow go out to face them, *for the LORD is with you*" (2 Chronicles 20:15, 17; emphasis added). Wow! I am speechless and grateful every time I read these words. This is my assurance, my safeguard. I serve a God who fights my battles. Replace the words "this great multitude" with whatever you are facing, and these verses will become your safe place to run to.

In response, the king and all his people bowed down and worshiped, and the Levites "stood up to praise the LORD . . . , with a very loud voice" (verses 18, 19). That's all they could do after they received God's marvelous answer. *But they hadn't won the battle yet.* All they got was a word from the Lord—and that was enough for them to start praising. They believed that it would happen just as He said. I want to do the same: to start praising while I am still in it, believing that God will find a way out because He fights my battles, and He is "power-full"!

When God heard their praises

The next day, as they went out to meet their enemies, "Jehoshaphat stood and said, 'Listen to me, O Judah and inhabitants of Jerusalem, *put your trust in the LORD your God and you will be established. Put your trust in His prophets and succeed.*' When he had consulted with the people, *he appointed those who sang to the LORD and those who praised Him in holy attire, as they went out before the army* and said, 'Give thanks to the LORD, for His lovingkindness is everlasting' " (verses 20, 21). Amazing! Truly amazing!

I love the king's reminder to everyone to trust the word of the Lord. When we trust Him, we confront our anxiety but with faith in His ability, not ours. Put your trust in the Lord and His Word. The battle will pass—in His way and in His time. Also, I am amazed that the singers went out in front of the army. Who goes into battle with a choir? God's people do. Simply because when we are powerless over the battle, we can still choose to raise our voices in praise, relying on Him to fight on our behalf.

"When they began singing and praising" (verse 22)—that's when God acted. The beginning of this verse is very significant. It was at the very moment of their praise that the Lord set ambushes against their foes. Their enemies destroyed each other, and when the people of Judah arrived, there were only corpses on the ground. It took three days for the king and his people to carry the spoil out because there was so much (verse 25). We, too, need to learn to start singing and praising, right now, in the middle of a dark situation. In the middle of sickness, in the middle of a relationship problem, in the middle of a financial spiral—we ought to raise our voices and tell God that we believe He will fight this battle for us.

Their return to Jerusalem was loud and joyful as they rejoiced over the victory God had accomplished (verse 27). They came to the house of the Lord with harps, lyres, and trumpets. *Their dreaded situation had turned into a flamboyant celebration.* They celebrated *before* and *after* the victory because they trusted in the word of their powerful God.

Stand and see His salvation

When sin entered this world, we became powerless over its consequences. Sin ruled in our minds and bodies. It seemed that we would forever be separated from God and were doomed to perish eternally. A *great multitude* of sins buried us and rendered us powerless. Yet Jesus came to live a perfect life in our place and, at the cross, gave up His perfect life, taking our place in death. He fought our battle and won. He died for our sins and purchased eternal life for us, even though we didn't deserve it. And, as Jehoshaphat and his people returned with a rich spoil—*which they had not earned*—we will live forever in the new earth without sin, death, or suffering (see Revelation 21:4), *which we did not earn. Jesus earned it for us.* And there is more: the same One who purchased our salvation also fights our daily battles. So be encouraged, and remember:

Lesson 9: Frequently, we face situations in which our strength and wisdom are not enough. Yet we have this assurance to rely on: though we are "power-less," our God is "power-full."

10

THE BATTLE OF RESOURCES

Lesson 10

"God with us" is the ultimate resource we can always count on. Don't be tempted to look for help in unhealthy alliances that offer false promises.

> *In the worst times we are to preach Christ, and to look to Christ. In Jesus there is a remedy for the direst of diseases, and a rescue from the darkest of despairs.*
>
> —C. H. Spurgeon,
> "Immanuel—The Light of Life"

Ahaz was one of Judah's wayward kings, prone to idol worship and other pagan practices. He declined God's offer of divine intervention and instead decided to seek help from Assyria. For a complete picture of the story, read Isaiah 7 and 2 Chronicles 28.

Where can we find help? What do we do when we're afraid? Who can rescue us? Parents are the main reliable resource for children in trouble. My parents saved my life many times when I found myself in a dire situation. In previous books, I have told of these experiences. One that stands out is when my mother took me, about four years old at the time, on a bicycle ride across fields in La Pampa, in Argentinian Patagonia. She had borrowed a bike and had placed a little seat for me behind her. As we were enjoying the scenery, the path got rough, and I had to straighten up. Without realizing it, I placed my foot inside the moving wheel. I started crying, and my mom stopped. When she took off my sock, a big part of my foot came off with it. The turning wheel spokes had chopped off my flesh; the bone was exposed. What to do next? There were no cellular phones, we were in the middle of nowhere, and I was bleeding. My mother sat me on the main seat of the bike, grabbed the handle, and ran several miles back to town. If not for my mother, I wouldn't be here. I was very young, so the foot "rebuilt" itself after several months, and I could walk again. My mother was a reliable resource; I knew she would save me, as always.

For adults, though, the question about reliable resources gets more complicated. We are more competent, more resourceful, but more distrustful. We look for resources anywhere and everywhere. The problem is that sometimes we find ourselves in situations that are way over our heads. And no human resource is sufficient. If you are there today, there is an amazing biblical narrative that we can learn from. It's the story of Ahaz, the king who chose his own resources over God's.

When our hearts shake

During the reign of Ahaz, king of Judah, the kings of Israel and Aram went to Jerusalem to wage war. "When it was reported to the house of David, saying, 'The Arameans have camped in Ephraim,' his heart and the hearts of his people shook as the trees of the forest shake with the wind" (Isaiah 7:2). Do you know that feeling? When you receive news that makes your heart shake as the trees of the forest shake with the wind? Where, then, should Ahaz go? How could he face this powerful alliance?

God immediately stepped in and gave the prophet Isaiah a message for King Ahaz. But before we discuss the content of this message, let me tell you a bit about this king. After David and Solomon's reigns, there were periods of revival and periods of decline in Judah. Some kings followed the Lord God of Israel (times of revival); others sacrificed to pagan gods (times of decline). Ahaz's reign was definitely a time of decline. "He [Ahaz] walked in the ways of the kings of Israel; he also made molten images for the Baals. Moreover, he burned incense in the valley of Ben-hinnom and burned his sons in fire, according to the abominations of the nations whom the LORD had driven out before the sons of Israel. He sacrificed and burned incense on the high places, on the hills and under every green tree" (2 Chronicles 28:2–4; see also verses 22–25). I am amazed that God still reached out to him in the moment of crisis, aren't you? We serve a God who never gives up, even on the worst among us.

Now back to the crisis. God said to Isaiah, "Go out

now to meet Ahaz, you and your son Shear-jashub, at the end of the conduit of the upper pool, on the highway to the fuller's field, and say to him, '*Take care and be calm, have no fear and do not be fainthearted because of these two stubs of smoldering firebrands*' " (Isaiah 7:3, 4; emphasis added).

Wow! First of all, God reached out to this evil king with a message of assurance and hope. Second, he even sent a "visual aid" with Isaiah—his son's name, *Shear-jashub*, means "a remnant will return," for God already knew the final outcome.

When Isaiah and his son approached him, the king might have been surveying the water reserves at the upper pool. And that is because water was one of their biggest problems when a powerful enemy threatened to surround Jerusalem. Though Ahaz had dishonored and betrayed the God of Israel, the Lord spoke to him in such a tender tone, telling him not to be dismayed because these two stumps of smoldering logs will not prevail against him. God presented Himself as Ahaz's main resource, the Source of all he may need. God offered a sure outcome, saying in no uncertain terms: "It shall not stand nor shall it come to pass" (verse 7). On the other hand, if Ahaz refused God's help, he would not last: "If you do not stand firm in your faith, you will not stand at all" (verse 9, NIV). A great advice for all.

The sign
Ahaz needed a little push to trust the Lord as his main

Source of strength and security. "Ask a sign for yourself from the LORD your God; make it deep as Sheol or high as heaven" (verse 11). Wouldn't you like such an opportunity—to ask God for a sign so that you can have absolute assurance of His presence? I would! "But Ahaz said, 'I will not ask, nor will I test the LORD!' " (verse 12). Sounds pious, but it's not. The truth is that he had other plans already. Ahaz had decided to find the "resources" he needed (see 2 Kings 16:7–9) in the king of Assyria (even though he would create a big problem for Ahaz's son Hezekiah once he ascended the throne). That's why he didn't want help from the Lord at this point. He was putting his trust in the alliance with Assyria. Sound familiar? Like Ahaz, we get so desperate that we start looking for resources anywhere and everywhere, and that's how we create bigger and bigger problems for ourselves. We are lured by unhealthy and false promises of rescue, even though God is offering us His limitless power.

Even though Ahaz refused to ask for a sign, the Lord gave him one anyway: "Therefore the Lord Himself will give you a sign: Behold, a virgin will be with child and bear a son, and she will call His name Immanuel. . . . For before the boy will know enough to refuse evil and choose good, the land whose two kings you dread will be forsaken" (verses 14, 15). *Immanuel*, God with us. You have heard this amazing prophecy during Christmas. We are not sure exactly how or through whom this prophecy was fulfilled in the time of King Ahaz.

But the ultimate fulfillment of this prophecy was Jesus, the true Immanuel—God with us. God came to dwell with us in the person of Jesus Christ. Matthew narrates the birth of Jesus as a direct fulfillment of this specific prophecy: "She will bear a Son; and you shall call His name Jesus, for He will save His people from their sins. Now all this took place to fulfill what was spoken by the Lord through the prophet: BEHOLD, THE VIRGIN SHALL BE WITH CHILD AND SHALL BEAR A SON, AND THEY SHALL CALL HIS NAME IMMANUEL, which translated means 'GOD WITH US' " (Matthew 1:21–23).

I like C. H. Spurgeon's words on the subject: "Surely this God-appointed sign was both in the depth and in the height above: the Man of sorrows, the Son of the Highest. This vision was the light of the age of Ahaz. It is God's comfort to troubled hearts in all the ages; it is God's sign of grace to us this morning. The sure hope of sinners and the great joy of saints is the incarnate Lord, Immanuel, God with us. May he be your joy and mine even this day."[1]

Jesus, God made flesh, came to live a perfect life in our place. He gave His perfect life as a sacrifice, at the cross, dying in our place. He felt abandoned because of our sin so that you may never feel abandoned. And He was raised from the dead on the third day. He is our assurance and guarantee of eternal life. This same God, who was willing to pay for your sins and transgressions, promises to be with us as our main source of strength, provision, and refuge.

Our Refuge

Not realizing that Assyria wasn't really a friend, Ahaz refused God's help. A few years later, Assyria would destroy many cities of Judah. Why not choose God instead of our own "Assyria"? God wants to be your defender. He is your source of strength and deliverance. You don't need to look anywhere else. Don't be tempted to make illicit alliances to defend yourself because God is your strength, and He has already secured the outcome. He says to you: Trust me; trust in God. He has saved you; He is your strength; He is your source. He provides all that you need, and He knows the future. He is our God, and we are His people. Don't go anywhere else seeking strength for your battles. And have no fear . . . for God is with us. "God is our refuge and strength, a very present help in trouble" (Psalm 46:1). Jesus assured us: "I am with you always, even to the end of the age" (Matthew 28:20). Woo-hoo!

Lesson 10: "God with us" is the ultimate resource whom we can always count on. Don't be tempted to look for help in unhealthy alliances that offer false promises.

---

1. Charles Haddon Spurgeon, "Immanuel—The Light of Life," September 14, 1890, *Metropolitan Tabernacle Pulpit*, vol. 36, The Spurgeon Center, https://www.spurgeon.org/resource-library/sermons/immanuel-the-light-of-life/#flipbook/.

11

THE BATTLE OF TRUST

Lesson 11

We are to trust the Word of the Lord above all others. And we must learn to ignore all the other voices that speak contrary to His.

> *You may safely rest in words* which urge you to faith in God. *Are you exhorted tonight to lay your burden of sin down at Jesus' feet? Obey such a word as that without questioning. You may well rest on words which bid you to believe in Christ, and you may, without fear, believe in him who has all grace and wisdom and power to save and to bless you.*
>
> —C. H. Spurgeon, "Words to Rest On"

This story takes place when Assyria has already taken the people of the northern kingdom of Israel into exile, and now Sennacherib, king of Assyria, is setting siege to Jerusalem. Hezekiah, king of Judah, must decide how to face this intimidation. For the complete story, see 2 Kings 18; 19.

After sixteen years in the business world, I was approached by the Seventh-day Adventist Church with a call to ministry. My career was well established, and I always thought I would do ministry as a volunteer. In fact, I had been volunteering as a youth minister throughout my sixteen years in business. I was surprised by the call but believed it was from God. Yet, some people tried to discourage me. One man tried to convince me that, as a woman in ministry, I would never amount to anything. I had a successful career in business, he said, and I wasn't making a wise decision, leaving all that for ministry. Nonetheless, I was convinced that this was a call from God, whether it made sense or not. I clearly remember my answer: "If the church gives me a little corner with a pulpit where I can preach the gospel, that's all I want."

Twenty-one years later, I am so thankful for the opportunity. I had to trust God's calling above all the other "logical" voices that tried to dissuade me from it. Yes! We are to trust God's Word above all other voices— no matter how much pressure those voices place on us or how much sense they seem to be making in our limited human minds. In this chapter, we will study a story from the life of King Hezekiah, who chose to trust God's Word above the *other* voices. And believe me, those other voices were quite loud!

It's not looking good

One of the laws of "systems thinking" in business is, "Today's problems are yesterday's solutions." This is significant. Sometimes we are surprised to see a problem arise out of the blue, but if we pay attention, we can often trace it back to the past when someone thought it would be a good solution for a pressing problem without realizing that this "solution" would create more problems later. And that's what happened to Hezekiah. His father, King Ahaz, had made an alliance with Assyria instead of relying on God (see the previous chapter). During Hezekiah's reign, Assyria turned against the kingdom of Judah, the same people that they once "helped."

Hezekiah was a king who did right in the sight of the Lord, removing the pagan places of worship (see 2 Kings 18:3–6). "He trusted in the Lord, the God of Israel; so that after him there was none like him among all the kings of Judah, not among those who were before him" (verse 5). "And the Lord was with him; wherever he went he prospered. And he rebelled against the king of Assyria and did not serve him" (verse 7). By the time we get to our story, Assyria had already taken the people of the northern kingdom of Israel into exile. Now, Sennacherib, king of Assyria, came against the fortified cities of the southern kingdom of Judah (see verse 13). Interestingly, the Assyrian records attest to this attack, more proof of the veracity of the biblical record. The Assyrian king boasted that he made Hezekiah a prisoner in Jerusalem "like a bird in a cage."

When the enemy came to conquer the city of Lachish, Hezekiah sent a message to the king of Assyria: " 'I have done wrong. Withdraw from me; whatever you impose on me I will bear.' So, the king of Assyria required of Hezekiah king of Judah three hundred talents of silver and thirty talents of gold" (verse 14). Hezekiah had to cut off the gold from the doors of the temple to meet the demands. Still, the king of Assyria sent his representatives with a large army to Jerusalem. It's fascinating that "they came and stood by the conduit of the upper pool, which is on the highway of the fuller's field" (verse 17); this is the place where Hezekiah's father, King Ahaz, had been met by Isaiah the prophet when he came with a message of comfort and help from God, which Ahaz refused, making an alliance with Assyria instead. Now, the same "friendly" Assyria was threatening Ahaz's son, Hezekiah. Yes, sometimes today's problems are yesterday's "solutions." And, in this case, it's not looking good.

Whom will you trust?
Will we trust God when circumstances are pointing in the opposite direction? This was a decision that king Hezekiah and his people had to make. We do too. The battle of trust takes place in our minds, even before we face our enemy.

What followed the army's arrival was intimidating ancient trash talk, for the Assyrians came with several arguments to try to dissuade Judah from trusting in God. The king of Assyria's messengers started with: "What is this confidence that you have? . . . Now on whom do you rely, that you have rebelled against me?" (verses 19–20). Verses 19–35 are incredible. They intimidated; they bargained; they even seemed to be aware of a prophecy against Judah because they claimed that Assyria was doing God's bidding: "Have I now come up without the LORD's approval against this place to destroy it? The LORD said to me, 'Go up against this land and destroy it' " (verse 25). They were definitely using heavy "artillery of intimidation."

Hezekiah's three representatives asked the Assyrians, "Speak now to your servants in Aramaic, for we understand it; and do not speak with us in Judean in the hearing of the people who are on the wall" (verse 26). But the Assyrians *wanted* the people to hear their threats, which got even bolder and meaner:

> Then Rabshakeh stood and cried with a loud voice in Judean, saying, "Hear the word of the great king, the king of Assyria. Thus says the king, 'Do not let Hezekiah deceive you, for he will not be able to deliver you from my hand; *nor let Hezekiah make you trust in the LORD, saying, "The LORD will surely deliver us, and this city will not be given into the hand of the king of Assyria."* Do not listen to Hezekiah, for thus says the king of Assyria, "Make your peace with me and come out to me. . . ." But do not listen to Hezekiah when he misleads you, saying, "The Lord will deliver us." Has any one of the gods of the nations delivered his land from the hand of the king of Assyria? . . . Who among all the gods of the lands have delivered their land from my hand, that the LORD should deliver Jerusalem from my hand?' " (verses 28–35; emphasis added).

Pretty intimidating words, aren't they? Perhaps you,

too, have felt the sting of words like those? Yet *before* our enemy taunts us, makes fun of us, and offers the most "logical" arguments, we need to decide in our hearts whom we will trust. And when someone verbally assaults us, we do well to learn from Judah's response: "But the people were silent and answered him not a word, for the king's commandment was, 'Do not answer him' " (verse 36). How I wish that I could tell you that I have remained silent every time somebody trash-talked me, even as my blood was boiling in my veins. Unfortunately, that's not the case. And, instead of sending someone to punch the trash-talker in the face, Hezekiah did what we all need to learn to do.

Spread your letters before God

What happened next is recorded in 2 Kings 19 and Isaiah 37. King Hezekiah humbled himself and "entered the house of the LORD" (2 Kings 19:1). He then called on the prophet Isaiah. The bottom line is that he sought the Lord. God has all the answers to our no-way-out situations. And if you have purposed in your heart to trust in Him, He will not disappoint you. Isaiah sent God's message to the king: "Thus says the LORD, 'Do not be afraid because of the words that you have heard, with which the servants of the king of Assyria have blasphemed Me. Behold, I will put a spirit in him so that he will hear a rumor and return to his own land. And I will make him fall by the sword in his own land' " (verses 6, 7). Well, that's good news, isn't it? Yet Assyria wasn't done yet. You know the type—very persistent trash-talkers.

King Sennacherib tried one more time, but now with a personal message to Hezekiah that defied God Himself: "Do not let your God in whom you trust deceive you" (verse 10). He went on to list all the nations that he had already conquered, pointing out that their gods did not prevent them from being destroyed by Assyria. Why would Judah be different? Oh! He was in for a surprise. He didn't know Yahweh, the God of Judah. And Hezekiah went directly to Him.

"Then Hezekiah took the letter from the hand of the messengers and read it, and he went up to the house of the LORD and spread it out before the LORD" (verse 14). I *love* this verse. He took the papers that the threats were written on, placed them in front of his powerful God, and prayed a beautiful prayer, which contains wonderful assertions about who Yahweh is: "You are the God, You alone, of all the kingdoms of the earth. You have made heaven and earth" (verse 15). He then said that, though Assyria had destroyed so many nations and their gods, "they were not gods but the work of men's hands, wood and stone" (verse 18). Then he made his specific petition for deliverance: "O LORD our God, I pray, deliver us from his hand that all the kingdoms of the earth may know that You alone, O LORD, are God" (verse 19).

I love the idea of "spreading our letters" in front of the Lord. I don't know what your letters are: divorce papers, a bad lab report, a notice of eviction, a final check from your job? Whatever they are, spread them before our God. Trust in Him, not in what you see or hear. He cares, and He acts on behalf of His people.

God's action

God answered immediately, through the prophet Isaiah, with a word against the king of Assyria. In 2 Kings 19:20–34, the Lord says that Sennacherib has "haughtily" lifted up his eyes against Him. Yes, Assyria had destroyed some fortified cities, but that was because God planned it that way, not because Assyria was greater than Israel's God. And God had plans for Sennacherib: "I will turn you back by the way which you came," says the Lord (see verse 28).

I am so encouraged that God always has the "big redemption picture" in mind. Not only would Assyria not conquer Jerusalem, but the Lord places this deliverance within the context of His covenant with Judah and the house of David:

"For out of Jerusalem will go forth a remnant, and out of Mount Zion survivors. The zeal of the LORD will perform this.

"Therefore thus says the LORD concerning the king of Assyria, 'He will not come to this city or shoot an arrow there; and he will not come before it with a shield or throw up a siege ramp against it. By the way that he came, by the same he will return, and he shall not come to this city,' " declares the LORD. "For I will defend this city to save it for My own sake and for My servant David's sake" (verses 31–34).

In His redemptive plan, God had already guaranteed that a remnant would come out of Judah. What is even more important is that through the line of David (Judah), the Messiah, Jesus Christ, would come to save the whole world. So, the outcome was guaranteed for us all. Amazing!

In just one verse, God takes decisive action, and the whole thing is over, trash talk and all. "Then it happened that night that the angel of the LORD went out and struck 185,000 in the camp of the Assyrians; and when men rose early in the morning, behold, all of them were dead" (verse 35). That's it. Day after day of threats, boasting against Yahweh, the God of Israel . . . all gone in one verse. The king of Assyria returned home to Nineveh, and there he was killed by two people who plotted against him.

Will you trust God, who created heaven and earth? Spread the letters of your circumstances before Him. He has already acted on your behalf, taking your place at the cross, purchasing the forgiveness of your sins and your eternal life with His spilled blood. He has already saved everyone who trusts in His sacrifice. In addition, He knows how many hairs you have on your head, how many problems you have in your hands, and how many burdens you carry in your soul. Accept Him as your

Savior and trust Him with your difficult situations. Spread your problems in front of Him. Only He has all power, grace, and provisions. He will guide you and deliver you. When facing a battle, always remember:

Lesson 11: We are to trust the Word of the Lord above all others. And we must learn to ignore all the other voices that speak contrary to His.

12

The Battle of Discouragement

Lesson 12
When circumstances are overwhelming, let God fight your battles. He will surely rescue you from distress and discouragement.

Nehemiah was well qualified for his work. He gave the Jews very shrewd, sensible, and yet spiritual advice, and this was a great help to them in their hour of need. Beloved, we have a better Leader than Nehemiah; we have our Lord Jesus Christ himself, and we have his Holy Spirit, who dwells in us, and shall be with us.
—C. H. Spurgeon, "The Two Guards, Praying and Watching"

This story takes place during the Persian rule of the ancient world. Nehemiah was the personal cupbearer of King Artaxerxes and led expeditions to Jerusalem to rebuild the walls of the city previously destroyed by the Babylonian armies. Read the full story in Nehemiah 1–6.

M y mind kept telling me that I was in trouble. Sometimes difficult circumstances may create a scenario so daunting that we are thrown into a dark pit. That's what happened to me in Cheltenham, United Kingdom. I am usually very positive and ready to tackle the task, no matter how hard. And that's the reason I was there to begin with. I was starting a PhD program at the University of Gloucestershire, United Kingdom. Much of my studies was going to be remote; I would do the research in the United States. But to start the program, my professor asked me to meet him in Cheltenham; I was to stay there for two weeks so that we could discuss the proposal for my research topic. I didn't have a lot of money, so I reserved a room at the YMCA. When I got there, accommodations were less than desirable, and I was cold and felt unsafe in my room.

The next day, I had to walk quite a distance to get to the university. The old campus buildings looked as if they had a long history. They felt quite intimidating, actually. I met my professor, and we discussed my topic. He gave me a couple of books to read and said that he would see me in two weeks. What? I thought we were going to meet often and that I would not spend the entire two weeks by myself in a place where I didn't know a soul!

As I started to read the books, I began to feel overwhelmed. They were very difficult, discussing research that was hard to follow. Everything started piling up, and I felt as if I were being swallowed up in a black hole. My usual positive self-talk turned dark: *What am I doing here? There's no way I will ever be able to research this topic. I'm never going to make it.* I was without family or friends, in a strange and unsafe place in a foreign country, without transportation, and stuck with my reading material. For the first time in a long time, I felt utterly discouraged. All I could do was cry out to my God for help. I knew that this was my calling and that He would have to give me insight and strength I didn't then possess. And He came through.

As I look back, my personal circumstances resembled those narrated in Nehemiah: "Then Judah said, '*The strength of the laborers is failing, and there is so much rubbish that we are not able to build the wall*' " (Nehemiah 4:10, NKJV; emphasis added). *I am not able . . . my strength is failing . . . there is so much debris that I can't see through this . . . I definitely can't do this.* Can you relate? If so, please keep reading. And let me tell you Nehemiah's story from the beginning.

Distress and reproach

One of his compatriots came from Judah to Susa, and Nehemiah eagerly inquired about Jerusalem and those who had survived captivity. The news was not good: "The survivors who are left from the captivity in the province are there in *great distress and reproach*. The wall of Jerusalem is also broken down, and its gates are burned with fire" (Nehemiah 1:3, NKJV). Not even a shadow of the splendor of Jerusalem remained, just rubbish and debris. The wall was down, the gates were burned, and the survivors were downcast. Nehemiah sat down to weep for many days. Do you know *that* feeling?

But he didn't only cry and mourn. He also fasted and prayed (verse 4). He was preparing to hear from God, to get some answers or instructions from Him. Prayer appears at many pivotal points in the book of Nehemiah (see Nehemiah 1:4; 2:4; 4:9; 5:19; 11:17; etc.). In chapter 1:5–11, Nehemiah prayed a gut-wrenching prayer of confession and sorrow for his sins and for those of his people, and he appealed to God's redemptive covenant with His people (verse 5, 10). He knew that this story was happening within the much greater story of redemption history; our story does too. Nehemiah asked God to hear his petition and grant him mercy in the sight of the king. At the end of chapter 1, we discover that Nehemiah was the king's cupbearer (verse 11).

In the fourth month after the initial prayer, an opportunity arrived. Finally—after four long months. I have learned that my calendar has never ever matched God's. His timing is not ours, so, before we even start, we need to decide to trust His timing, not ours.

God's good hand

When the time is right, everything happens fast and effortlessly because His providence is leading. The king inquired about Nehemiah's sadness (Nehemiah 2:2). And for the first time, Nehemiah told him: "May the king live forever! Why should my face not be sad, when the city, the place of my fathers' tombs, lies waste, and its gates are burned with fire?" (verse 3, NKJV). He had kept his sorrow secret for four months, and now everything came out at once. The king responded with a question: "What do you request?" (verse 4, NKJV). What an opportunity!

Before answering, even though he had been thinking about it for four months, *he prayed again*. Then he boldly requested: "If it pleases the king, and if your servant has found favor in your sight, I ask that you send me to Judah, to the city of my fathers' tombs, that I may rebuild it" (verse 5, NKJV). Nehemiah was the cupbearer, mind you. But he was willing to become a construction foreman if that's what God wanted. He planned to rebuild the wall. With what building experience, I don't know. He asked not only for time off to do this task but also for the king's letters to permit him to pass through other regions to get to Judah. Also, he wanted timber to make beams for the gates, for the city wall, and for the residence where he would be staying. He requested materials for three projects. Big plans! And—the king granted it all. Woo-hoo!

Nehemiah attributed the king's willingness to one main reason: "According to the good hand of my God upon me" (verse 8, NKJV). Countless times I have known in my heart that something was happening only because I have the favor of God in my life. I have His good hand upon me. And I am so grateful. Are you convinced that you have the good hand of your God upon you? Nehemiah was, and so he went on his way to rebuild the wall of Jerusalem. But when he got there, he realized soon enough that not everyone was happy about his building projects.

Here comes trouble

Opposition came quickly: "When Sanballat the Horonite and Tobiah the Ammonite official heard of it, they were deeply disturbed that a man had come to seek the well-being of the children of Israel" (verse 10, NKJV). Later on, a third opponent appeared, Geshem the Arab (see Nehemiah 2:19). Opposition from the north, the east, the south. Corralled from all sides. Sound familiar?

Yet Nehemiah chose to focus on that which God had put in his heart. He surveyed the damage, and then he gave a testimony:

> And I told them of the hand of my God which had been good upon me, and also of the king's words that he had spoken to me.
> So they said, "Let us rise up and build." Then they set their hands to this good work (verse 18, NKJV).

Testimonies about God's past acts on our behalf are powerful, and they motivate us even under dire circumstances. And that's what happened to Nehemiah's people: once they heard Nehemiah's side of the story, they were ready to start rebuilding.

But the opposition wasn't ready to let them do it. They laughed, they despised, they questioned (see verse 19). Nevertheless, Nehemiah kept focusing on his God and the task at hand. He answered his enemies: "The God of heaven Himself will prosper us; therefore we His servants will arise and build, but you have no heritage or right or memorial in Jerusalem" (verse 20, NKJV). I admire Nehemiah's focus. He wasn't about to spend time or energy pondering his adversaries' comments. One of the best insights that I have ever received is this: you empower that which you give energy to. So, choose wisely. Whatever you spend time thinking about, that will grow in your mind. Nehemiah chose to focus on God, His power, and His plans, not on the opponents' words, mockery, and threats.

A time to build, pray, and guard

The opposition intensified: "Now it came about that when Sanballat heard that we were rebuilding the wall, *he became furious and very angry and mocked the Jews*" (Nehemiah 4:1; emphasis added). Their enemies were now angry; the mockery went to a different level. "Tobiah the Ammonite was near him and he said, 'Even what they are building—if a fox should jump on it, he would break their stone wall down' " (verse 3). Even worse, all the enemies got together to plan on fighting against Jerusalem (verse 8). These challenges started piling up, getting into the builder's heads little by little. Nehemiah, as always, started praying. He honestly told the Lord that they were despised and that their enemies' mockery and threats were demoralizing the builders (see verses 4, 5). Even though they had built the wall all around to half of its height (verse 6), their souls were bruised from all the mockery, ridicule, and threats.

Discouragement started building up, day after day. That's how we usually find ourselves in the midst of the battle of discouragement. We are not usually discouraged on the first day or when we hear the first dissenting voice. But as the days go by, more voices oppose, more adverse circumstances pile up, and it doesn't improve.

Then little by little, discouragement can take hold of our hearts. And that's how we get to the verse mentioned in my introductory story:

> "The strength of the burden bearers is failing,
> Yet there is much rubbish;
> And we ourselves are unable
> To rebuild the wall" (Nehemiah 4:10).

Too much debris left behind by all the destruction, too much trash lying around, and our strength is failing.

Nehemiah was a great leader. He kept praying and working. He is a model of *active trust* or *trust in action*: he knew that God's favor was upon him, he prayed constantly, *and* he also did what was in his power to do. He prayed and then set guards over the wall. "Then I stationed men in the lowest parts of the space behind the wall, the exposed places, and I stationed the people in families with their swords, spears and bows" (verse 13). Yet by now, his men were not only discouraged but fearful. Nehemiah stepped up to the occasion: he trusted God, prayed, took action, *and* also led, motivating his people with two core reminders. First, he reminded them how great their God was; second, he told them to focus on the reason they were doing this—their families. "When I saw their fear, I rose and spoke to the nobles, the officials and the rest of the people: *Do not be afraid of them; remember the Lord who is great and awesome, and fight for your brothers, your sons, your daughters,* your wives and your houses" (verse 14; emphasis added).

Perhaps you need to be reminded of the same today: you have an awesome, caring, and powerful God, and you have a purpose in life. Pray, and then go change another diaper. Pray, and then go feed your aging parent. Pray, and then go preach another gospel sermon. Pray, and go do what you must do. You are not on your own. You have an awesome God who has given you an awesome purpose, and He will give you the means and the strength to accomplish the task before you.

Nehemiah explained: "From that day on, half of my servants carried on the work while half of them held the spears, the shields, the bows and the breastplates. . . . Those who carried burdens *took their load with one hand doing the work and the other holding a weapon*" (verses 16, 17; emphasis added). I don't know about you, but I am pretty impressed with their multitasking. I am impressed with your multitasking, too: as a single parent, as a caregiver, as a parent of a child with special needs, as the person in charge, whatever your challenge is. I know what it's like to wear many hats. Yet, we are never alone. We have a great and awesome God.

Our God will fight for us

The most important part of Nehemiah's motivational speech was the words "our God will fight for us" (verse 20). No matter how prepared and skilled they were, the bottom line was that the battle wasn't theirs to win but the Lord's. They were His agents. You are

His agent. And He will guide you for His name's sake.

When the enemies realized that the wall was being finished, they changed tactics. They summoned Nehemiah, thinking that if they could stop the leader, the whole project would halt. But Nehemiah was not about to fall into their trap. The way that he answered is a motto for me when adversaries try to stop me from my calling: "So I [Nehemiah] sent messengers to them, saying, '*I am doing a great work and I cannot come down. Why should the work stop while I leave it and come down to you?*' " (Nehemiah 6:3; emphasis added).

God strengthened and defended Nehemiah and his people. The wall, which at one point looked impossible to build, was built in fifty-two days (see verse 15). And I love Nehemiah's conclusion of why this was possible: "When all our enemies heard of it, and all the nations surrounding us saw it, they lost their confidence; *for they recognized that this work had been accomplished with the help of our God*" (verse 16; emphasis added). It was God who accomplished it. All the credit was for the Lord.

Later on in the book of Nehemiah, you will discover a revival of their faith. The people turned back to the God of their ancestors. Their story was actually taking place within a much larger story of God's covenant of redemption. Out of Judah would come the Redeemer, Jesus Christ. God personally guaranteed the pact that He had made with humankind. At the cross, He fought on our behalf, dying in our place; He fought and won our salvation. Furthermore, He will fulfill His covenant of coming back to take His people to live with Him forever.

Are you facing discouragement due to your daily battles? Surrender these battles to Him, the One who has already purchased your salvation. He will make a way, whether that is guiding you with His providence, giving you strength, teaching you to multitask, or keeping your adversaries at bay. No matter what the battle is, you are not alone. Nehemiah was a great prayerful and motivational leader, yet our Leader is even greater. As the introductory statement by Charles Spurgeon highlights, "Nehemiah was well qualified for his work. He gave the Jews very shrewd, sensible, and yet spiritual advice, and this was a great help to them in their hour of need. Beloved, we have a better Leader than Nehemiah; we have our Lord Jesus Christ himself, and we have his Holy Spirit, who dwells in us, and shall be with us."

Whenever you start feeling discouraged, pray to your awesome God, who fights on your behalf. Let me share with you a secret: when the battle is too great, then it's not yours to fight. It's the Lord's. And remember:

Lesson 12: When circumstances are overwhelming, let God fight your battles. He will surely rescue you from distress and discouragement. Woo-hoo!

A FINAL NOTE
FROM ELIZABETH

Dear Friend,

Thank you so much for taking this journey with me. By now, I'm sure you've realized that the truth captured in this book—that *the battle belongs to the Lord*—has become very personal for me and is ingrained in my soul. I wrote this book in the midst of one of the fiercest battles I have ever faced. I believe every word I wrote. I often go back to the biblical narratives to remind myself how God intervened on behalf of His people to encourage my heart time and time again. Our God today is the same God of the Bible, and He still fights our battles here and now.

I trust that in considering the struggles of the biblical characters, you were reassured about God's love for you. God cares deeply for us, even though we are broken, frail, and flawed human beings. Our weaknesses and powerlessness are the very reason we need a Savior. And before finishing this book, I invite you to receive Jesus as your personal Savior. I encourage you to trust that, at the cross, He redeemed not just the whole world but *you* personally. When you accept His sacrifice on your behalf, *your* sins are forgiven, no matter how heinous they may be, because He took your place. From that point on, you are covered with His perfection and assured of eternal life. He walks with us, and we are never ever alone.

At the end of this book, you will find an offer for free Bible studies. We would be delighted if you join us to learn more about our awesome Savior.* We want to share with you the good news of Jesus and the difference He makes in our daily lives. He is coming soon to take us home, a place without battles, suffering, or death. I can't wait to be there!

He secured our salvation, and He also fights our daily battles. We usually see that best when we are at the end of our rope, having run out of all resources or answers, and He surprises us with His divine intervention. I invite you to surrender your life to Him and become His disciple. When you face your own battles, which all of us do in this sinful world, you can be assured that as a child of God, you will never face these battles on your own. The mighty God, Creator of heaven and earth, intervenes on your behalf daily just as He did at the cross to secure your eternal salvation.

---

* To access more content by Elizabeth Talbot, visit Jesus101.tv for daily devotionals, videos on demand, audiobooks, daily Bible study podcasts, and much more.

This book has shown that no matter what battle you are facing—an impossible situation, a lack of understanding, detours or mistakes, feeling left out, fear, comparing yourself with giants, exhaustion, not seeing God's viewpoint, being powerless over a situation, having limited resources, facing intimidation, or just feeling discouraged—God fights on your behalf for the battle belongs to the Lord! You are never alone.

> He who did not spare His own Son, but delivered Him over for us all, how will He not also with Him freely give us all things? . . . Who will separate us from the love of Christ? Will tribulation, or distress, or persecution, or famine, or nakedness, or peril, or sword? . . . But in all these things we overwhelmingly conquer through Him who loved us. For I am convinced that neither death, nor life, nor angels, nor principalities, nor things present, nor things to come, nor powers, nor height, nor depth, nor any other created thing, will be able to separate us from the love of God, which is in Christ Jesus our Lord (Romans 8:32–39).

Woo-hoo!

Be blessed, my friend; I leave you in the most capable hands in the universe.

Until next time,
Elizabeth

For additional FREE resources, videos on demand, daily devotionals, biblical studies, audiobooks, and much more, please visit our website:

www.Jesus101.tv

If you have been blessed by this booklet and would like to receive free Bible Studies, please contact us through our website or write to us at

Jesus 101 Biblical Institute
PO Box 10008
San Bernardino, CA 92423

WATCH the JESUS 101 channel on ROKU!

DOWNLOAD the JESUS 101 app TODAY!